menu planning:

a blueprint for better profits

menu planning:

a blueprint for better profits

HUBERT E. VISICK & PETER E. VAN KLEEK

McGraw-Hill Book Company

New York
St. Louis
San Francisco
Düsseldorf
Johannesburg
Kuala Lumpur
London
Mexico
Montreal
New Delhi
Panama
Rio de Janeiro
Singapore
Sydney
Toronto

Library of Congress Cataloging in Publication Data

Visick, H E
Menu planning.

1. Food service. 2. Menus. I. Van Kleek, Peter E., joint author. II. Title.
TX943.V57 642'.5 72-14109
ISBN 0-07-067063-3

Hubert E. Visick received his formal training at Brigham Young University and Utah State College. After eight years as a teacher and principal, he entered the fields of hotel management and foodservice, becoming Manager of the Zion Canyon Lodge and Executive Assistant to the General Manager, Sun Valley, Idaho. Later he became Supervisor of Operating Departments, Eppley Hotels Company, Omaha, Nebraska, a position he held for ten years. He was responsible for controlling food, liquor, and labor costs; for planning menus; and for controlling the quality of food and service. For the last eleven years of his life, he was Merchandising Manager for Foster Lunch System, Ltd., in San Francisco, and during this time he also became an accredited instructor at City College of San Francisco, where he taught menu planning classes in the Hotel and Restaurant School for nearly four years.

Peter Van Kleek is a graduate of the School of Hotel Administration at Cornell University and is a member of the Cornell Society of Hotel Men. Before becoming an Associate Professor of Food Service in the Vocational Division of the State University of New York at Alfred, he applied his training as manager for several hotels such as the Barringer Hotel in Charlotte, North Carolina and the Jack Tar Hotels, Galveston, Texas; he also was Leasor-Operator of the Mimosa Inn in Tryon, North Carolina. His *Anthology of Vegetable Cookery* is published and used by the Community Colleges of North Carolina.

Menu Planning: A Blueprint for Better Profits

567890EBEB798

The editors for this book were Ardelle Cleverdon and Alice V. Manning, the designer was Marsha Cohen, and its production was supervised by James E. Lee. It was set in Versatile 53 by University Graphics, Inc.
It was printed and bound by Edwards Brothers Incorporated.

contents

preface

WHY STUDY MENU PLANNING?

Success in the business of selling food is directly proportionate to the quality of planning involved and inversely proportionate to the amount of guesswork used in lieu of planning.

A menu without selling prices wouldn't make much sense. Neither would a menu without known costs make sense. How do you know what the selling price should be unless you know the costs? Not just the food cost—all the costs!

You cannot know what the food cost will be unless you can control production and purchasing. You cannot know what the wage cost will be unless you know how much labor is required to produce and serve the items on your menu.

To make a profit, you must plan for a profit. There can be no guesswork about either costs or selling price. The study of menu planning involves determining costs and controlling them. It includes the techniques of fixing selling prices.

The menu is the center of your food operation. A poorly planned menu can:

Increase your food cost
Add to your cost of labor
Complicate your purchasing
Upset your kitchen
Destroy your service
Drive customers away
Reduce sales volume

. . . and, consequently, make it impossible to realize a profit from your operation.

Menu planning also includes selling techniques and merchandising know-how. It involves knowledge of color, design, layout, type faces, printing, and lithography; it requires familiarity with grades and types of paper. A good working knowledge of culinary terms and menu language is also needed.

A menu planner must also know methods of food preparation and all types of service. He must be familiar with food production equipment and serving equipment. He also needs a knowledge of food purchasing and equipment buying. He must be conversant with flavors, spices, seasonings, garnishes, appearance, and taste of many food products. He needs basic knowledge of nutrition and dietetics.

Menu planning is a function of top management not to be left to those who have neither adequate knowledge nor sufficient interest. The menu should be the first step in planning a new restaurant. It is the document upon which the plans, equipment, and furnishings are based.

It is, therefore, a necessity to have a thorough working knowledge of the art of menu planning to be successful in the competitive food industry of today.

A NOTE ABOUT HUBERT E. VISICK

The food industry and educational field will greatly miss Mr. Visick. He had outstanding knowledge of the industry, great interest in people and was much in demand as an able and interesting speaker and advisor. He coordinated the recent session of the Council on Hotel and Restaurant Industry Education.

In recent years Mr. Visick was able to return to his early career and deep interest in teaching, becoming a member of the faculty of the Hotel and Restaurant School of the City College of San Francisco. In this capacity he prepared the manuscript for his book "Menu Planning—a Blueprint for Better Profits." After its private printing in October of 1967 it became the textbook of the Menu Planning Class at City College of San Francisco and also is used at Disneyland University. Without advertising or fanfare the book was enthusiastically received by both educators and executives in the industry as a clear and concise study of menu planning, the key to good restaurant operation.

Peter E. Van Kleek

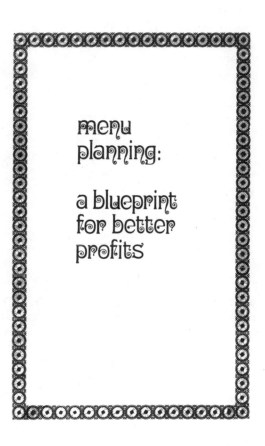

menu planning:

a blueprint for better profits

1.

The Menu Planner as a Person & When to Plan

The importance of menu planning to the success of any foodservice establishment cannot be overemphasized. The individual doing the planning is influenced by his own attitude toward food, his knowledge of food, his imagination, and his creative ability. Most important, he should have a deep interest in food.

It is important that the menu planner be free of prejudices and food dislikes. An example of this is a person who does not like variety meats of any type—for example, liver, kidneys, tongue. Many types of variety meats are perfectly acceptable on most menus, and in some restaurants they are demanded by the customer. The planning of a menu should not be regarded as a routine duty but as an opportunity to present a three-dimensional picture of food—beautiful to look at, nutritionally sound, and delightful to taste.

To plan a menu takes time, interest, ability, and knowledge. It is an exact science, and it is the difference between profit and loss in the foodservice industry.

The planning of a menu should not be hurried, and the time for it should be budgeted by management. There is no set length of time required to plan a menu, but whatever time it does take should be considered well spent.

Not only management but also the operating department head must take an interest in planning good menus. It is management's responsibility; however, the chef is responsible for its production, the steward for the raw materials, the headwaiter for its service, and the accountant for its feasibility (whether it will be profitable).

Careful thought is essential if the menu planner is to be able to recognize whether an item is salable and, if so, whether it can be sold at a profit. The knowledge the menu planner must have is varied, but there are certain essentials; he must know (1) the likes and dislikes of the potential customer, (2) the availability of raw materials, (3) the ability of the production and service personnel, and (4) the limitations of the equipment and space of the foodservice establishment.

One of the questions that immediately comes to mind concerns how often a menu should be changed. There is no set answer, because the situation varies from restaurant to restaurant. In the cuisine restaurant, the menu is the basic theme of the establishment, and much effort has been put into the planning of it. Once a menu item becomes a slow seller or a nonprofitable item, it should be reevaluated and a change made. This does not mean that the whole menu should be replaced, but that a new item should be substituted for the nonseller or the prices restructured. Management should review the menu regularly and make necessary changes.

Do not avoid changes just because you have a large supply of preprinted menus on hand. Your investment in printed material is small compared with your investment in the continuing success of your place of business.

In the writing of cycle menus, there is no fixed number of days that make up a cycle. In some institutions there are four cycles a year to reflect the four seasons. Each one of the seasonal cycles may be broken down into smaller cycles of thirty days or seven days. The object of a cycle menu is to give the consumer a prepared variety that does not reoccur at noticeable intervals. The cycle menu will also facilitate purchasing, storage, recipe standardization, and profit planning.

Many operators do not like cycle menus and insist on a daily menu. The reason they most often give for this is that their customers demand it. Other reasons are that they can take advantage of good food buys and can utilize their leftovers this way. With intelligent planning, a cycle menu can be instituted which will be acceptable to the customer and also take advantage of food that is seasonable and in good supply. Leftovers can be eliminated with intelligent planning of controls and production.

It takes time to plan a good menu; therefore it should not be done during the food preparation time. The menu planner must take into consideration what is available in the refrigerator, but the menu should not be just a reworking of yesterday's failures or leftovers.

If at all possible, the menu should be planned during an uninterrupted time in an office away from noise, confusion, and the aromas of cooking food. The office should have menu forms, standardized recipe files, a dictionary, cookbooks, and other sources of ideas such as foodservice periodicals. A file of previous menus is essential. Your food thoughts are generally influenced by the food you have most recently eaten and the mood you are in. Arrange the day so that you will have menu planning time when you are fresh and, most important, free from interruptions. Give yourself ample time to do a thorough job.

REVIEW QUESTIONS

1. The individual doing menu planning is influenced by attitudes, knowledge, and ability. Discuss how your own attitude toward food could affect planning a menu.
2. Whose responsibility is it to plan menus for a restaurant?
3. What specific knowledge must the menu planner have to plan menus that will be acceptable to the public and also generate a profit?
4. Why are cycle menus used in many places of business?
5. At what time of day should a menu be planned and under what conditions?

2.

TYPES OF FOOD-SERVICE ESTABLISHMENTS AND THEIR MENU REQUIREMENTS

There are many types of food establishments, and each has its own requirements for menu planning. This unit will deal with the divisions of the foodservice industry and the requirements of each segment. Let us first consider the three major divisions: institutional, industrial, and commercial. Each has its own characteristics; however, there is one major difference, and that is the profit motive. Institutional foodservice establishments serve food out of necessity. Industrial facilities are motivated by necessity in some cases but are mostly operated for convenience. The commercial restaurant is operated to serve a single purpose, and that is to make a profit for the investor.

INSTITUTIONAL FOODSERVICE

The institutional segment may be further divided into schools (grade schools, high schools, community colleges, and residential colleges); hospitals, mental institutions, and nursing homes; and the armed services. Each institutional facility has its own menu or diet requirements. However, the one basic factor that has to be taken into consideration in planning the menu is that it must be nutritionally sound.

The following must also be taken into consideration in planning a menu for any one of the institutional facilities:

1. Type of facility
2. Ages of the people consuming the food
3. Budget requirements
4. Food likes and dislikes of the consumer
5. Location of the institution
6. Equipment of the facility
7. Type of service required
8. Hours of feeding
9. Availability of skilled labor
10. Storage facilities
11. Governmental regulations
12. Religion and ethnic background
13. Esthetic value of the food
14. Competition

Feeding in the grade school and high school is governed under the National School Lunch Act of June 1946, Public Law 396. In more recent years, other laws have been enacted by Congress which provide for matching funds, a federal milk program, and the commodities distribution program. In planning a school lunch menu, the A lunch, which is a nutritional pattern set by the USDA, must be followed. The A lunch pattern is as follows:

1. Two ounces edible portion of lean meat, poultry, or fish; or 2 ounces cheese; or one egg; or 1/2 cup cooked dried beans or dried peas; or 4 tablespoons peanut butter; or an equivalent quantity of any combination of the above-listed foods
2. A 3/4-cup serving of two or more vegetables or fruits or both, full-strength vegetable or fruit juices being allowed to meet not more than 1/4 cup of this requirement
3. One slice of whole-grain or enriched bread or a serving of corn bread, biscuits, rolls, or muffins made of whole-grain or enriched meal or flour
4. Two teaspoons of butter or fortified margarine
5. One-half pint of unflavored fluid whole milk as a beverage

For the community college, on a one-meal basis, the following should be provided in the menu:

1. Two cups of milk
2. Two ounces of lean meat, or its equivalent
3. One serving of citrus fruit or other fruits or vegetables that are a good source of vitamin C
4. One serving of dark green or yellow vegetables for vitamin A
5. One serving of other vegetables, including potatoes
6. Two slices of whole-grain or enriched bread, or 3/4 cup of cooked cereal, or the equivalent in other grain products
7. Two teaspoons of butter or fortified margarine
8. One serving of liver or other meat high in iron content at least once a week

In a residential college, you have the additional responsibility of planning nutritionally balanced menus that encompass three meals a day over an extended period. The essential dietetic requirements of this age group are:

1. Four or more 8-ounce servings of milk daily
2. Two or more servings of 3 ounces of lean cooked beef, veal, lamb, pork, or fish; two eggs; one cup cooked dried

beans or peas; 4 tablespoons peanut butter; or the equivalent
3. Four or more 1/2-cup servings of fruits and vegetables per day, including one serving of citrus or other vitamin C fruits or vegetables; one serving of dark green or yellow vegetables high in vitamin A; two or more servings of vegetables or other fruits, including potatoes
4. Four or more servings of one slice whole-grain or enriched bread; 1 ounce of ready-to-eat cereal, or 3/4 cup cooked cereal or enriched grain products
5. Two teaspoons of butter or fortified margarine
6. One serving of liver or other meat high in iron at least once a week

In writing menus for the other institutional facilities (hospitals, nursing homes, mental institutions, etc.), the minimum daily requirements should also be followed. However, the need for special diets is always present, such as soft, full, liquid, clear liquid, or salt-free. To plan hospital and other institutional menus, it is recommended that further study be given to normal and therapeutic nutrition.

INDUSTRIAL FOODSERVICE

Industrial feeding would be described as employee feeding by industry. This segment may be broken down into three categories, as follows:

1. Company-owned or company-subsidized
2. Leased
3. Vending

The main reason for an industrial plant to have a food facility is to provide the workers with good food at reasonable prices in a short period of time. Menu planning for industrial cafeterias or restaurants has much in common with that for commercial establishments. However, an emphasis must be placed on the following factors:

1. The work the employee does—whether he is in management, is an office worker, or does physical labor

2. Time period allotted for the meals
3. Prices compatible with wages or salaries
4. Number of shifts and length of shifts
5. Space available for the cafeteria or restaurant facilities
6. Kitchen and serving facilities
7. Potential number of persons to be served and whether they want full-service menus or only partial menus (to supplement food brought from home)
8. The company's attitude toward subsidy loss in the foodservice area; whether it should be a "break-even" menu
9. Competition by other food facilities located near the industrial plant

COMMERCIAL RESTAURANTS

The major portion of the foodservice industry covers the profit-oriented restaurant. For menu planning purposes, let us break down restaurants into the following categories:

1. Full service
2. Cuisine
3. Cafeteria
4. Drive-in
5. Specialty restaurant
6. Nationality restaurant
7. Hotel (American plan and European plan)
8. Catering establishment (on or off the premises)

If you were to separate them by price range, the lower-cost facilities would comprise coffee shops, diners, cafeterias, and drive-ins. Another major consideration in planning menus for the low price range is usually that they are fixed menus, with a la carte pricing, selective clip-ons, and sometimes a daily special plus full lunch or dinner menu.

Restaurants in the medium price range are generally specialty, nationality, and full-service dinner houses catering to the middle class. The menu generally has a fixed price for a complete meal, along with an a la carte listing.

Some restaurants will have a bar operation, and this will influence menu planning in that the restaurant will depend on a large share of revenue from beverages rather than food. The menu should contain broiled items, such as steaks and chops, which are compatible with alcoholic beverages. Some of the most popular specialty houses are as follows:

1. Steak or beef
2. Chicken
3. Fish
4. Nationality, e.g., French, Spanish, Italian, Mexican, German, Chinese

High-priced or cuisine-type restaurants can be in hotels, single-unit operations, or chain operations. They may be of any nationality; however, the majority are French in origin. They may have a French or Russian service, with some cooking or finishing of the product done in the dining room, either by the waiter captain or by the chef. The menu is generally priced a la carte, but fixed-price, full-dinner menus will be encountered. Such restaurants normally tend to serve two meals a day, lunch and dinner or dinner and supper.

A major portion of the foodservice industry today is the fast-food or franchised restaurant. We treat them in this book as a separate entity because of their marked differences from the rest of the restaurant industry. They are different in many ways, particularly with regard to:

1. Strictly a la carte pricing
2. Limited menus
3. Frequent lack of a dining room
4. 24-hour-a-day operation in some cases
5. Tendency to use paper and plastic ware
6. Limited number of employees, most being in the production area
7. Take-out business
8. Fast service or self-service
9. Menu almost completely based on convenience foods

The most popular of the franchised or specialty drive-in restaurants are hamburger, hot-dog, chicken, barbecue, dairy-type, nationality, and pancake houses.

REVIEW QUESTIONS

1. If commercial restaurants are operated for a profit, why are institutional and industrial facilities operated?
2. List ten factors that must be taken into consideration in planning menus for institutional facilities.
3. What must be included in a class A school lunch to provide the nutritional requirements of school-age children?
4. Industrial foodservice facilities serve a varied market. Many factors must be taken into consideration in planning their menus. List the five factors that you think are most important.
5. Survey your community and list the restaurants, classifying them as to type.

3.

The Menu Form

Throughout history, the menu has taken a form based on how the consumer eats. For example, on a breakfast menu you would not list fish and then juice, because traditionally people consume their juice first. Therefore, it becomes important to know the form for the various meal periods. The breakfast form of an a la carte or table d'hote menu is given in Example 1:

Example 1

Juices and fruits
Cereals
Egg dishes
Griddle
Meats
Vegetables
Breads
Beverages

Simple lunch and dinner menus should be in the form of Example 2:

Example 2

Appetizer
Entree
Vegetable
Starch
Salad
Bread
Dessert
Beverage

If only these two forms were used, menu planning would be relatively simple. As the menu is developed, however, you find you are adding choices to each area, such as orange juice, prunes, and baked apples in the appetizer section of the breakfast menu. Which do you list first, and why? Some menu planners will do this by pricing, but it is preferable to follow what is called the classic menu pattern. Basically, the menus of the Western nations are the same, with a few minor exceptions, but the Eastern and Far Eastern are very much different.

In this book we will deal with the Western menu. To help

clarify the finer breakdown of the classic menu, Example 3 lists the breakdown for the classic breakfast pattern. Example 4 is the developed classic luncheon menu. Example 5 is the full dinner menu in the classic pattern. For the cuisine restaurant, the American-plan hotel, the steamship lines, or the dinner house, a slightly different pattern evolves, as seen in Examples 6, 7, and 8.

Once you are familiar with the menu form, planning the menu becomes relatively simple provided that you have the background knowledge of food and sources of food information readily available.

The menu planner should also be prepared to write children's menus as an aid to better merchandising in his restaurant. Four points must be taken into consideration in planning the children's menu.

1. The likes and dislikes of two- to twelve-year-olds
2. The amount of money the parent is willing to spend for the child's dinner
3. The nutritional needs of the child
4. What the parents consider good for the child (see the example of a well-balanced children's menu on page 28)

There are a number of restaurants in large cities that feature a supper menu or after-theatre menu. In planning the supper menu, the following should be considered:

1. Hours of service (generally 11 p.m. until closing)
2. Additional labor cost involved
3. Price range that will be acceptable to your customer
4. The frame of mind of the guest, i.e.,
   a. Is it a major meal for him?
   b. Is it a snack meal?
   c. Is it an accompaniment to alcoholic beverages?
   d. Is it a combination of a late dinner and early breakfast?

An example of the all-purpose supper menu will be found on page 29.

Another type of menu that is found in the catering department of hotels and restaurants is the brunch menu. This is a combination of breakfast and lunch, usually served between 11 a.m. and 1 p.m. In recent years, it has become increasingly popular as a prime meal on Sundays. Many hotels or clubs use it to merchandise the normally slow after-church hours. One way they have found to promote it is by serving champagne with it. It may be either a buffet or a served meal. On page 30, you will find an example of a buffet brunch menu.

With the emphasis today on portion control, generally restaurants are using the same portion size for both table d'hote and a la carte menus. Many times the menu price for the a la carte will be slightly higher to induce the sale of the complete dinner and increase the average check.

An example of a commercial hotel a la carte breakfast menu may be found on pages 31 to 32. Note the number of items offered. On pages 33 to 34 is a fixed luncheon menu. This is an example of a type of menu that is favored by a large number of restaurants catering to business people; it gives a choice of entree but no choice of vegetable or accompanying items. On pages 35 to 37 there is an a la carte luncheon menu with many choices.

The menu planner must have a complete knowledge of the skills and abilities of the preparation and service personnel. It would be foolish to place an item on the menu that neither the cook could prepare nor the waiter properly serve.

Keep planning, testing, and adding to your menu. Eventually, you will have a customer-accepted menu that is a profit builder.

Example 3

	BREAKFAST		
JUICES AND FRUITS	Fruit or Vegetable Juice		
	Fresh Fruit		
	Stewed Fruit		
CEREALS	Cold		
	Hot		
EGGS AND OMELETS	Baked	Poached	Fried
	Scrambled	Shirred	Sauces
	Omelet	Plain	
		Filled	
GRIDDLE	Pancakes		
	Waffles		
	French Toast		
	Scrapple		
MEATS	Bacon	American	Canadian
		Irish	
	Ham	Steak	Sugar Cured
		Baked	Country

	Sausage	Country	Pork
		Link	Variety
	Beef	Steak	Creamed
		Hash	Chipped
	Variety meats	Calves Liver	Chicken Liver
		Kidneys	
	Fish	Fresh	Salted
		Smoked	
VEGETABLES	Potatoes	Fried	Hash Brown
	Tomatoes		
	Grits		
BREADS	Toast		
	Variety Breads		
	Sweet Breads		
	Pastries		
BEVERAGES			

Example 4

	LUNCHEON	
APPETIZERS	Juices	Fruit
		Vegetable
	Fruit	
	Cocktails	Meat
		Poultry
		Fish
SOUP	Hot	
	Cold	
ENTREES	Hot	Meat
	Cold	Poultry
		Fish
		Eggs
		Meat Substitute
VEGETABLE		
SALAD	Accompaniment	
BREADS		
DESSERTS		
BEVERAGES	Coffee	
	Tea	
	Hot Chocolate	
	Milk	
	Soft Drinks	

Example 5

		CLASSICAL
APPETIZERS	Juice	Fruit
		Vegetable
		Other

	Fruit		
	Hors d'Oeuvres	Vegetables	
		Starch	
		Fish	
		Poultry	
		Meat	
SOUPS	Fruit		Hot
	Vegetable		Cold
	Poultry		Clear
	Fish		Heavy
	Meat		Chowders
			Bisques
			Cream
			Puree
			Garnish
ENTREES	Fish	Whole	Broiled
	Shellfish	Steak	Baked
		Filet	Sautéed
			Fried
			Poached
			Sauce
			Garnish
	Poultry	Turkey	Hot, Cold
		Chicken	Roast
		Duck	Fried
		Variety	Poached
			En Sauce
			Accompaniment, Garnish
	Meats	Beef	Hot, Cold
		Veal	Roast
		Lamb	Baked
		Pork	Broiled
		Variety	Grilled
		Meat Substitutes	Sautéed
			Poached
			En Sauce
			Accompaniment, Garnish
	Game	Fish	Hot, Cold
		Bird	Grilled
		Flesh	Roast
			Baked
			Broiled
			Sautéed
			Poached
			En Sauce
			Accompaniment, Garnish
VEGETABLES	Green	Strong, Mild	Poached
	Yellow	Starchy, Non-starchy	Broiled
	Red		Baked

	White		Sautéed
	Fresh		Fried
	Pastas		Sauce, Garnish
SALADS	Fruits	Hot, Cold	Poached
	Greens	Starchy, Non-Starchy	Broiled
	Vegetables		Baked
	Meat		Sautéed
	Poultry		Fried
	Fish		Sauce, Garnish
	Cheese		
	Starch		
BREADS	Rolls	White	
	Slices Bread	Whole Wheat	
	Biscuits	Rye	
	Muffins	Graham	
	Sweet Breads	Cornmeal	
		Oatmeal	
		Flavors	
		Spice	
		Herb	
		Nuts	
		Fruits	
DESSERTS	Cakes		
	Tortes		
	Cookies		
	Meringues	Fruit	
	Pies	Nut	
	Tarts	Custard	
	Pastries		
	Custards	Fruit	
	Puddings	Nut	
	Creams		
	Ices	Fruit	
	Fruits	Fresh	
		Stewed	
	Cheese	Imported	
		Domestic	
BEVERAGES	Coffee	Variety, Original	Garnish
	Sanka	Hot, Cold	
	Tea		
	Postum		
	Milk		
	Hot Chocolate		

Example 6

<u>AMERICAN</u>

APPETIZERS	Juices
	Fruits
	Cocktails
	Hors d'Oeuvres

SOUPS	Clear Thick Cold
FISH	Freshwater Saltwater Shell
EGGS	
ENTREES	Beef Veal Lamb Pork Poultry Variety
GRILLS	
VEGETABLES	Green Yellow Red Starchy
POTATOES	
DINNER SALADS	Green Vegetable Fruit
COMPOTES	Fresh Cooked
DESSERTS	Baked Frozen
CHEESES	Sharp Mild
BEVERAGES	

Example 7

FRENCH

HORS D'OEUVRES	Meat	Fish	Poultry	Vegetables	
SOUPS	Clear	Heavy			
EGGS	Hot Cold				
FISH	Baked Broiled Poached	Shell	Whole	Steak	Filet
ENTREES	Beef Veal Lamb Pork Variety Poultry	Roasted Poached			

VEGETABLES	Green Yellow Red Starchy		
PASTAS	Grain variety		
GRILLS	Meat; Poultry		
COLD BUFFET	Plate Meat		
SALADS			
CHEESES	Sharp Mild		
DESSERTS	Baked Frozen		
STEWED FRUIT			
FRUIT	Melon	Citrus	Berry
INFUSIONS OR BEVERAGES	Hot Cold		

Example 8

	ITALIAN		
APPETIZERS	Juices Fruit Cocktails		
HORS D'OEUVRES	Fish Meat Poultry Eggs Vegetable	Hot Cold	Raw Cooked
SOUPS	Clear, Creamed		
FARINACEOUS OR PASTAS			
FISH			
ENTREES			
GRILLS			
ROASTS			
VEGETABLES			
POTATOES			
COLD BUFFET	Sauces		
SALADS			
CHEESES			
DESSERTS			
ICES			
FRUIT	Fruits in Syrup	Dried	Fresh
BEVERAGES			

Example 9

SPANISH

JUICES
COCKTAILS
SOUPS
SEAFOODS
POULTRY
MEAT
EGGS
RICE
PASTAS
VEGETABLES
SALADS
SWEETS
FRUIT
CHEESES
BEVERAGES

REVIEW QUESTIONS

1. What is the classic menu pattern for breakfast?
2. Using the classic lunch menu pattern, write a class A school lunch menu.
3. How do the French and the American classic dinner menu patterns differ?
4. Select a menu from a restaurant in your community and evaluate it as to conformity with the basic menu pattern.
5. Write a simple brunch menu containing only one entree.

4. Physical Characteristics of a Good Menu

A menu is not merely a list of items for sale like a parts catalog; it is the most important merchandising tool available for a restaurant.

It must therefore list the foods in an appetizing manner, using terms which are easily understood by the customer. It should harmonize with the atmosphere of the restaurant and help to create a desired image.

There is a very little reason, except possible snob appeal, to write a menu in French or any other foreign language. There is, however, a very good reason to call sauces, methods of preparation, and names of dishes by their proper names, whether in French or English or another language.

Fish should be listed as fish, not as poisson; however, it is acceptable to list filet of sole Marguery, if the sauce Marguery is described.

The menu planner must consider the potential customer and his knowledge of food. Most guests would recognize the term New York strip steak, and the only other explanation needed would be the quality, such as prime or choice. However, not all your customers read French or other foreign languages; consequently, when listing foreign terms, such as beef ragout, a simple explanation is needed, such as "a traditional French beef stew, cooked in red wine with garden-fresh vegetables."

Whether to use descriptions or more austere listings is a matter of individual preference. It is important to use good taste and honesty in describing your offerings. Flowery phrases do not improve the quality of poor food.

Generally speaking, fine restaurants and dining rooms use very limited descriptions, if any, while less expensive restaurants and coffee shops go in for more descriptive language.

A working knowledge of menu terms and culinary language is essential for good menu writing. However, restraint should be exercised in its use. Remember the purpose of the menu is to present the articles you have for sale in an appetizing manner, in language which is easily understood. The use of a dictionary is recommended, and the menu planner should have the ability to express himself in proper English. The most common mistake made in translation is the proper placement of the adjective. In English, it is generally placed before the noun.

There are many types of menus: a la carte, table d'hote, semi–a la carte, limited table d'hote, etc. The type of menu is fixed by management policy. We shall discuss advantages and disadvantages in a later unit.

The menu must tell the customer what he will get and what he will pay for it in clearly stated language which cannot easily result in his confusion or embarrassment.

How long should a menu be? How many items should be listed?

Most successful restaurants use limited menus. There are notable exceptions, some establishments offering very long menus and others using menus with only one or two entrees. Usually coffee shops list more items than the dinner houses. Again, it is a matter of personal preference as well as economy and efficiency of operation.

It is easier to teach proper preparation and correct service of a few items. On restricted menus, every item can become a specialty of the house.

SIZE

The menu should be large enough to carry your sales message in easily read type, without clutter or crowding. It should be small enough to be easily handled at the table. It should not be clumsy nor so small as to be ridiculous. Menus are usually folders or cards, but they can just as well be pamphlets or novelty shapes which lend themselves to specialty restaurants.

There are many sizes used by successful restaurants. A standard size is the 9 × 12 inch single-folded menu cover that either is printed on the inside cover or has a printed insert. The 8 × 11 inch single sheet has been a popular size for many restaurants.

MATERIALS

There is a great variety of paper of varying weights and different finishes. Thickness of paper is designated by weight, that is, 100-pound paper is thicker than 80-pound paper.

Toughness, durability, appearance, and finish depend upon what the paper is made of and how it is processed.

Slick finishes are thought to shed dirt and soil and so last longer. There is little advantage in having a slick outside finish which resists soiling if the inside finish is absorbent and untreated. A menu which is clean outside and soiled inside is unacceptable.

Menus should be varnished, after being printed, to make them soil-resistant.

Generally speaking, slick finishes are used in drive-ins and less expensive restaurants. They are not considered suitable for fine dinner houses or good service restaurants.

It is often good practice to use a tough stock for the outside cover. Then print your menu on a lighter paper and fasten it in the cover. The menu can be changed without throwing away the costly covers.

There are papers and cover stocks for every purpose. Don't try to become an expert on paper. Select a well-qualified printer and rely on him for information and advice.

Color is a matter of good taste. It should be harmonious with the decor and pleasing to the eye. If you don't understand color, ask someone who does, preferably a professional. Don't go to extremes with some startling combination of garish, unappetizing colors. Color can also be expensive; added colors increase the cost of printing. Good color pictures require lithography and color separation.

Colors, pictures, and designs done by an amateur usually look amateurish. If your restaurant needs a menu, it needs a well-designed menu, and this requires the service of an artist who is experienced in menu design.

Many artists, because of their interest in effects, have little interest in economy. Discuss costs with the artist and the printer together before the design develops into a creation you can't afford to print. Hand lettering requires special plates and costs more than type-set lettering. It is also costly to change. Type-set letters and prices are easily changed.

There are dozens of type styles and faces available. Ask your printer about them, and he'll help you select artistic as well as practical types.

Inside the menu, the type should be easily read and graceful in appearance. An overcrowded menu is difficult to read no matter what the type face. There should be plenty of white space. It makes the menu attractive and easier to read and understand.

Of course, there is much planning to be done before writing a menu. All menus need to be carefully planned, even those which are not printed. Cafeterias will normally have menu boards, and these should be as well planned and attractive as the printed menu.

All-important is the fact that the menu should reflect the character of the restaurant. This is important in the original design. Are the dishes listed in keeping with the decor and theme of the restaurant? Does it reflect the atmosphere? As an example, an expensive restaurant will not have a cafeteria bulletin board for the menu. In writing the menu, the menu planner should not abbreviate. One very common error is the term "french fry." French-fried what? If you mean potatoes, spell it out!

The menu must be clean and current. Torn and dirty menus misrepresent your operation, unless it is also dirty. Clip-ons may be used, but only to sell current specials. If the clip-on is just another menu item, why wasn't it included in the original menu? If you are using preprinted menus, prices should not be constantly written over. If you are going to vary your menu prices, order preprinted menus where you can type in prices, or order small-quantity printing and change prices on your new print job.

The menu should provide basic information about the restaurant. Include its address, name of the city and state, phone number, days and hours of operation, what credit cards are honored, and what facilities it has.

Your menu is a great merchandising tool. Use it well, but remember its primary purpose is to sell the item the chef has prepared. It is the printed picture of your restaurant.

The following selection of sample menus covers a wide range of different meals in different types of restaurants.

THE WELLHOUSE RESTAURANT

Children's Menu

THE SPACE MAN
$.65
Peanut Butter Sandwich
Celery or Carrot Sticks
Milk
Ice Cream or Jello

THE MOONBEAM
$.95
Spaghetti & Meatballs
Coleslaw
Rolls & Butter
Milk
Ice Cream or Jello

THE RACER
$1.10
Fried Chicken Drumsticks
Mashed Potatoes
Green Beans
Rolls & Butter
Milk
Ice Cream or Jello

THE RIFLEMAN
$1.00
Hamburger on a Bun
French Fried Potatoes
Applesauce
Milk
Ice Cream or Jello

Supper Menu, Served Nightly 10 p.m.–2 a.m.

THE TOWN HOUSE

21 East Street

Kane, N.Y.

London Broil, Served on Homemade French Bread	*$3.75*
Tournedos Rossini	*6.50*
Veal Holsteiner Schnitzel	*5.50*
Pan Sautéed Chicken Livers a la Burgundy	*3.00*
Shirred Eggs with Canadian Bacon	*2.75*
Eggs Benedict	*3.50*

CHOICE OF THREE

Minted Green Peas	*Broiled Tomatoes*
Homefried Potatoes	*Mashed Potatoes*
Tossed Salad	*Tomatoes and Onions Vinaigrette*

Banana Flambé (for two)	*3.00*
Charlotte Russe	*1.50*
Crêpes Suzette (for two)	*3.50*
Meringue Glacé	*1.25*
Fresh Fruit and Cheese Platter	*1.50*

CHOICE OF:

Coffee *Tea* *Milk*

THE HOGBACK HOUSE
Tryon, N.C.

Sunday Champagne Brunch Buffet
Served 11:30 to 2:30
$3.50 per person

Chilled Melon
Blueberries in Cream
Fresh Strawberries
Choice of Juice

Eggs Mimosa
Eggs Benedict
Eggs Florentine
Bourbon Baked Country Ham
Beefsteak en Brochette
Bacon
Sausage
French Pancakes with Orange Syrup
Pecan Waffles

Brussels Sprouts in Celery Sauce
Fried Green Tomatoes
Buttered Grits
Country Fried Potatoes

Toasted Homemade Bread
Hot Biscuits
Sugar Cake

A la Carte

FRUITS AND JUICES

Orange Juice	*25–45*	*Grapefruit (half)*	*25*
Tomato Juice	*25*	*Stewed Prunes*	*25*
Pineapple Juice	*25*	*Sliced Bananas with Cream*	*35*
Kadota Figs	*35*	*Baked Apple*	*30*

Fresh Fruit (in season) 40
with Cream 35¢

FRESH, CRISP CEREALS

Kellogg's Corn Flakes *Pep (wheat flakes)* *Kellogg's 40% Bran Flakes*
Rice Krispies *Sugar Frosted Flakes* *Special K (protein cereal)*
Shredded Wheat *All-Bran* *Kellogg's Raisin Bran*
OK's (New Oat Cereal) *Cooked Cereal*

FROM THE GRILL

Bacon	*.60*
Premium Ham, Side Order	*.95*
Ham Steak	*2.50*
Grilled Sausage	*.90*
Fresh Eggs (2) (as you like them)	*.55*
Fresh Eggs (2) with Bacon, Ham, or Sausage	*1.00*
Jelly or Cheese Omelet	*.70*
Ham or Spanish Omelet	*.80*
Corned Beef Hash .75 with Poached Egg	*1.00*
Home Fried, Hashed Brown, or Lyonnaise Potatoes	*.30*
Broiled Sal Mackerel with Hashed Brown Potatoes	*1.00*
One Egg (to order)	*.30*
One Egg with Bacon, Ham, or Sausage	*.75*
Creamed Chipped Beef, Toast Points	*1.00*
Canadian Bacon and Eggs	*1.30*
Philadelphia Scrapple with Sautéed Apples	*1.00*

HOT CAKES, TOAST, AND ROLLS

Griddle or Buckwheat Cakes	*.45*	*Sweet Roll*	*.25*
Waffle with Syrup	*.45*	*Toast, Dry or Buttered*	*.20*
Milk Toast	*.35*	*Cinnamon Toast*	*.25*
Muffins (2)	*.20*	*English Muffin (1)*	*.20*
Fresh Doughnuts (2)	*.20*	*French Toast with Jelly*	*.55*

BEVERAGES

Fresh Hot Coffee .10 pot	*.20*	*Ice Cold Guernsey Milk*	*.20*
Hot Tea	*.15*	*Hot Chocolate*	*.25*
Postum	*.20*	*Sanka*	*.25*

Skim or Buttermilk .15

LOW-CALORIE
HIGH-PROTEIN BREAKFAST
(less than 400 calories)
Orange Juice
Special K
Protein Cereal with Milk
Sunrich Toast (1 slice)
Black Coffee
75¢

FOR KIDS
(of all ages)
Chilled Juice
Sugar Frosted Flakes
One Slice of Toast
with Jelly
Hot Chocolate, or Milk

75¢

Room Service Charge 25¢ per Person

LUNCHEON TODAY

French Fried Eastern Scrod with Tartar Sauce *Hashed Cream Potatoes and Cucumber Slaw Salad*	*$1.75*
Sirloin of Beef—A Roast Noted for Its Fine Flavor *Dill Buttered Potatoes and Asparagus Tips*	*2.10*
Cheese Soufflé with Tomato Sauce *Buttered Green Beans and Cucumber Slaw Salad*	*1.40*
Imported Canadian Bacon with Mustard Sauce *Golden Corn and Pineapple-Date Mallow Salad*	*1.80*
Stouffer's Salmon Loaf with Creamed Pea Sauce *Dill Buttered Potatoes and Green Snap Beans*	*1.55*
Chicken Fricassee over Toasted Noodles *Buttered Asparagus Tips and Spring Radishes*	*1.70*
Soup 'n' Sandwich Luncheon *Bowl of Creamed Mushroom Soup served with a* *Chopped Ham and Mustard Sauce Sandwich on Rye Bread*	*1.25*

Steaks and Loin Lamb Chops are always available

LOW-CAL LUNCHEON

Roast Sirloin of Beef *Fresh Asparagus Tips, Melba Toast, Chilled Melon, Coffee*	*2.60*

DESSERTS

Frosted Daiquiri Pie in Vanilla Crust			*.35*
Butterscotch Pecan Chocolate Cake			*.35*
Warm Apple Pie	*.35*	*a la Mode*	*.50*
Chilled Melon			*.40*

Ice Cream with Frosted Cake Square	*.35*
Prune Whip with Custard Sauce	*.30*
Peanut Toffee Sundae	*.35*
Fresh Strawberry Sundae	*.35*
Ice Cream or Fruit Sherbet	*.30*
Selection of Cheese with Toasted Wafers	*.45*

A LA CARTE MENU

Soup du Jour 25¢ Cup	*15¢*	*Melon Boat*	*40¢*
French Onion Soup au Gratin	*35¢*	*Cream of Tomato Soup*	*30¢*
Fresh Shrimp Cocktail	*75¢*	*Spring Vegetable Soup*	*30¢*
Chilled V-8 Juice	*20¢*	*Chilled Fruit Cup*	*50¢*
½ Grapefruit Supreme	*45¢*	*Chilled Pineapple Juice*	*20¢*
King Crabmeat Cocktail	*85¢*	*Canapé of Sardine*	*60¢*
Cantaloupe	*25¢*	*D.C. Bouillabaisse en Marmite*	*50¢*
Honeydew Melon	*35¢*		

SEAFOODS

Fillet of Sole, Tartar Sauce	*$1.10*
Broiled Lake Trout, Lemon	*1.65*
French Fried Jumbo Shrimp, Cocktail Sauce	*1.50*
Casserole of Fresh Crabmeat au Gratin	*1.85*
Flame Grilled Lake Superior Whitefish, Tartar Sauce	*1.65*

French Fried Potatoes *Tossed Salad Bowl*

Hot Rolls *Coffee*

LUNCHEON STEAKS—CHOPS—FOWL

Broiled Top Sirloin Steak	*$1.65*
Calves' Liver Sauté, Bacon	*1.50*
One Broiled Lamb Chop, Jelly	*1.65*
Creamed Chicken a la King en Casserole	*1.25*
Grilled Hamburger Steak, Grilled Onion	*1.25*
Flame Grilled Pork Tenderloin, Applesauce	*1.35*

French Fried Potatoes *Tossed Salad Bowl*

Hot Rolls *Coffee*

SANDWICHES

Baked Ham	*$ .50*	*Denver*	*$ .45*
Hamburger	*.50*	*Sliced Chicken*	*.85*
Toasted Cheese	*.35*	*Decatur Club Sandwich*	*1.00*
Swiss Cheese	*.30*	*Bacon-Tomato, Toasted*	*.45*
Smoked Liver Sausage	*.45*	*Chicken Salad*	*.60*
Hot Corned Beef	*.50*	*Chef's Special Sandwich*	*1.25*
Sardine Grilled	*.60*	*Peanut Butter-Bacon*	*.35*
Marshall Field	*1.25*	*Roast Sirloin of Beef*	*.65*
Smoked Beef Tongue	*.45*	*Bacon and Egg*	*.50*

Grilled Tomato, Bacon, and Cheese on Toast *.65*

DESSERTS

Mint Stick, Chocolate Chip, Strawberry Ice Cream	*20¢*
Sundae	*25¢*
Ice Cream and Cake	*30¢*
Pineapple, Orange, Lime Sherbet	*15¢*
Pie	*20¢*
A la Mode	*10¢ extra*
Parfaits: Chocolate, Butterscotch, Strawberry	*30¢*
Sliced Oranges	*25¢*
Sliced Pineapple	*25¢*
Half Peaches	*25¢*
Camembert Cheese	*35¢*
Liederkranz Cheese	*35¢*
Roquefort Cheese	*35¢*

Toasted Wafers served with Cheese

BEVERAGES

Coffee 10¢ Iced Coffee 10¢ Tea, per Pot 10¢
Sanka Coffee 10¢ Iced Tea 10¢ Postum 10¢
Milk Shake 25¢ Sweet Milk or Buttermilk 10¢
Chocolate Malted Milk 30¢ Chocolate Milk 10¢
Ginger Ale with Lime Sherbet 30¢

REVIEW QUESTIONS

1. What type of foreign terms would be acceptable in an American menu?
2. Using the classic menu pattern referred to in Unit 3, write a seven-day-cycle for an industrial cafeteria.
3. Plan an a la carte coffee shop luncheon menu.
4. What are the physical characteristics of a good menu?
5. Design a menu cover for a steak house.

5.

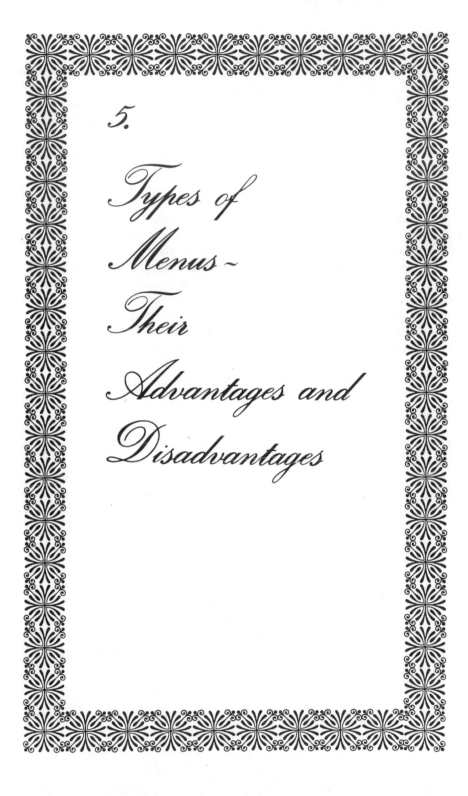

Types of Menus— Their Advantages and Disadvantages

A la carte menus are those which price each item separately. Very few truly a la carte menus are in use today. In some expensive restaurants, a la carte pricing is accepted. Customers who patronize these restaurants are not concerned particularly with prices.

Most customers prefer a menu on which it is easy to see what they will get and what they will pay for it.

Many restaurant operators think that it is easier to control costs when an a la carte menu is used. It is true that it is easier to calculate cost. However, this is a poor reason to use any type of menu. The menu you want is the one your customers prefer. No menu is good unless it pleases the customer.

It is probably true that restaurants using a la carte menus have lower food costs than those using other types of menus. Where each item is priced separately, it is frequently priced higher, hence a lower cost percentage. Most customers resist a la carte pricing; they are more conscious of prices when each item is priced separately. They do not like having to add up several items to find how much lunch will cost.

A low food cost isn't a great advantage, of course, if you don't have customers or if a high labor cost is created by the menu choice.

The extreme opposite of the a la carte menu is the table d'hote menu. A table d'hote menu offers a complete meal at a fixed price.

Years ago, these menus included appetizers, soups, fish, poultry, beef, or other red meats, several potatoes, three or four vegetables, salads, breads, desserts, beverages, and liqueurs.

The table d'hote menu served on the West Coast

*

Morro Bay Shrimp Cocktail — *California Fruits au Kirsch*
Freshly Squeezed Orange Juice — *Chilled Tomato Juice*

*

Lobster Bisque — *Chicken a la Reine*
Consommé Madrilène

*

Poached Filet of Pacific Sole Marguery

*

Roast Capon with Chestnut Dressing
Broiled Nevada Lamb Chops, Mint Sauce
Roast Sirloin of Beef au Jus
Baked Virginia Ham, Champagne Sauce
Asparagus Spears Hollandaise *Potatoes Parisienne*
Early June Peas au Beurre *Duchess Potatoes*

*

Limestone Lettuce, Vinaigrette

*

Assorted Rolls and Butter

*

Biscuit Tortoni *Coupe St. Jacques*
French Pastries
Compote of Fruit *Strawberry Tart*
Chocolate Sundae

*

Café Noir

$7.50 Per Person

To project the costs of this menu, you need to know the sales and mix. After discovering (by experience over a reasonable period) the average number of orders of each item sold, you can determine the mix and thus be reasonably accurate in precosting.

Customers seem to like the table d'hote menus. They feel they are getting a lot of food for their money. They also like this type of menu because it tells them exactly what they will get and what they will pay for it. Customers also like the freedom to choose among several items at one price.

Increasing costs have forced price increases. Resulting prices of complete table d'hote menus have exceeded the popular price range. Today's customers are no longer willing to pay the price of a really complete menu.

Restaurant operators have come up with several variations of the table d'hote menu in an effort to offer attractive combinations at attractive prices.

In some cases, the menu has been shortened. Usually the fish course is eliminated. Apppetizers and soups are priced a la carte. Desserts are also priced separately. The result is a semi–a la carte menu. The salad is sometimes served as an appetizer. Entrees are usually priced separately.

A semi–a la carte menu

*

California Orange Juice 50¢ *Chilled Tomato Juice* 40¢
Broiled Florida Grapefruit au Rum 75¢
Budega Bay Shrimp Cocktail 95¢ *King Crab Cocktail* 95¢
Consommé Diable 50¢ *Chicken Gumbo Soup* 50¢

Prime Rib of Beef au Jus	*$4.50*
Broiled New York Cut Sirloin Steak (12 oz.)	*5.00*
Roast Young Modesto Tom Turkey, Stuffing	*3.75*
Filet of Petrale Sole Marguery	*3.25*

(Price of the entree includes Salad, Potato, Vegetable, and Beverage)

Tossed Salad with French Dressing

*

Baked Idaho Russets *Whipped Potatoes*
Glazed Tiny Carrots *New Peas au Beurre*
Assorted Rolls and Butter
Coffee *Tea* *Milk*

*

Chocolate Parfait 65¢ *Wild Blackberry Sundae* 60¢
Apple Pie 40¢ *Pumpkin Pie* 40¢
German Chocolate Cake 50¢
Creme de Menthe 65¢ *Creme de Cacao* 65¢

Others have simply shortened the menu by eliminating some courses, by restricting selections of appetizers and desserts, or by limiting the selection of entrees to less expensive dishes. Thus, they are able to offer a limited table d'hote menu, moderately priced.

Limited table d'hote menu

Fruit Cup
Choice of Lettuce and Tomato Salad or
Soup du Jour

*

Pot Roast of U.S. Choice Beef Jardinière
Breaded Veal Cutlet, Tomato Sauce
Fried Chicken Southern Style, Country Gravy
Broiled Halibut Steak, Butter Sauce

*

Snowflake Potatoes *Green Beans and Bacon*

*

Apple Pie *Ice Cream* *Sherbet*
Coffee *Tea* *Milk*

$3.00 Per Person

Care must be used not to cheapen the menu in order to meet what seem to be popular prices.

Another version of the limited table d'hote menu follows:

Crisp Green Salad Topped with Shrimp

*

Top Sirloin Steak Maitre d'Hotel
Veal Scallopini a la Marsala
Plump California Chicken Sauté Sec
Filet of English Sole Bonne Femme

Spring Garden Peas with Tiny Onions
Baked Idaho Potato with Sour Cream and Chives
Assorted Rolls

*

Wild Mountain Blackberry Parfait
or
Creamy Cheese Cake

*

Coffee

$6.00 Per Person

This menu offers attractive choices but limits them enough to allow us to offer this good menu at a reasonable price.

Many restaurants, especially the better-class coffee shops, list a specific potato and/or vegetable with each entree, the purpose being to avoid serving unnecessary vegetables and to gain better control over quantities to be prepared. The entree with the vegetable or potato or both is priced separately. Usually beverage is included—but all other items are a la carte.

Another semi–a la carte menu

*

Tomato Juice 50¢
California Fruits au Kirsch 85¢
Consommé Supreme 45¢
Bisque of Crab, Cup 60¢
Crisp Greens topped with Shrimp $1.05

*

Roast Sirloin of Beef au Jus $5.00
with New Potatoes and Green
Beans Amande

*

Creme de Menthe Sundae 75¢

Vanilla Ice Cream 50¢
Wild Blackberry Parfait 65¢
Creme de Menthe 65¢
Fruit Sherbet 50¢
Chocolate Sundae 65¢
Creme de Cacao 65¢

There are many ways of arranging a menu. Some offer advantages to the restaurant. These are desirable if they do not take advantage of the customer or try to confuse him by trickery. A good menu states plainly what the customer will get and what he will pay for it.

Few successful restaurants offer a wide variety of a la carte entrees and other items. You can no longer afford to carry a number of items in stock on the chance that someone will order them. Neither can you afford the extra cooks and kitchen people needed to prepare special a la carte dishes.

There are restaurants which still write a menu every day, usually one for lunch and another for dinner. This is done in the belief that better variety can be provided by this method.

This is not always true. Careful analysis of the so-called daily menus covering a period of several weeks almost always reveals a repetitive pattern. Usually this pattern follows the days of the week. Thus, Thursdays tend to become like other Thursdays and Mondays like other Mondays. So, the excuse of providing better variety is not always valid.

Chefs and supervisors sometimes contend that menus written every day allow better flexibility. This is true—but the flexibility is used in working off leftovers which should never have become leftovers.

There are built-in faults in the daily menu system. Generally there is very little planning of the daily menus. They are left to the last minute and hurriedly put together. Purchasing is hit or miss, and there is no chance for precosting. Formulas are almost never used.

Many chefs and so-called food men cling to the daily menu

plan simply because they do not want to be pinned down. Under a system which requires planning, coordinated purchasing, precosting, and use of formulas, their lack of preplanning will always result in a higher labor and food cost.

If daily menus are written far enough ahead (five to ten days) to permit precosting, sales analysis, planned purchasing, and preparation of formulas, the system works well. Reevaluation and elimination of slow movers should be done frequently.

Cycled menus are planned for one week, two weeks, or any period of time, and the cycle is repeated over and over. This system permits better planning. The entire cycle of menus can be precosted before going into use. Formulas can be provided and tested and used over and over on a regular cycle. Purchasing specifications can be established, and purchasing can be done on a cycle too.

The cycled menu provides better variety because variety is planned into the cycle. Only the most popular items are written into the cycle.

From the customer's viewpoint, variety consists of several items he likes on each menu. The point is that variety cannot be provided by offering unpopular items, no matter how many you offer. Five popular entrees which most of your customers like provide far better variety than twenty-five entrees of which only three or four are popular. Careful study of customer preference is essential to good menu planning.

Another advantage in cycled menus is that they permit better training of cooks, waiters, pantrymen, and all others who prepare or serve your food. By repeating the items in a cycle, preparation and service should become progressively better.

Sales figures must be watched constantly. Unpopular items must be promptly replaced. New items should replace the less popular items, and there should be continuous programs of new product development. Only those new products which have been sales-tested and have proven popular should be used.

Some dinner houses serve the same menu every day—day after day. Such menus are composed of carefully selected items which are almost universally popular. Each is carefully prepared and carefully served. Each is really a specialty of the house.

The type of menu best suited to your restaurant depends upon the type of clientele you serve. If you can accurately appraise their preferences and their needs and plan a menu to suit them, you are half way to success. The other half consists of setting standards and training personnel to fulfill them.

REVIEW QUESTIONS

1. Write a dinner a la carte menu for a restaurant using the classic form. Menu suggestions may be taken from Unit 17.
2. Using the classic menu form, write a table d'hote menu for a hotel luncheon menu.
3. Why is the table d'hote menu preferred by most restaurant guests?
4. What information must you have to project the cost of a table d'hote menu?
5. List the advantages and disadvantages of writing your restaurant menu daily.
6. Explain the cycle menu.

6.

MENU PLANNING AND PURCHASING

The purpose of operating a restaurant is to make profits. The purpose of menu planning is to plan a profit.

It is hard to believe that in many restaurants, menus are not planned—they are simply written out of the refrigerator. Perhaps it would be more accurate to say that menus are written by the ice box. The "chef" sees chickens which are past their prime and starting to smell, so he puts barbecued, disjointed chicken on the menu. The hamburger (ground beef) looks pretty gray, so he adds a meat loaf. The leftover prime rib from three days ago is now good for only hash, so Southern beef hash appears. The leftover peas, limas, string beans, and carrots are combined as mixed fresh vegetables. This may be a little extreme, but look for it the next time you are in a kitchen where menus are written daily. This is not the case with all daily menus, but it is particularly true in many restaurants that have poor management or indifferent personnel.

Skill at working leftovers is not a substitute for good menu planning. A properly run kitchen has no leftovers. They are used before they are leftovers—the key is planning, planning to prepare and/or purchase only the quantities which will be sold when they are fresh.

This isn't the way a lazy restaurant runs, but it is the way a profitable restaurant operates.

WHO SHOULD PLAN THE MENU?

Most restaurants leave menu planning up to the chef. There seems to be no good reason for this. His knowledge of what competitors offer is limited, and his knowledge of what potential customers are buying elsewhere is restricted, therefore he needs help and guidance from management.

Menu planning is the function of top management along with the chef, or, if the size of the operation will justify it, a specialist whose background qualifies him as a menu planner. Assuming that the menu planner has access to all cost figures and is familiar with the profit and loss statement, he should plan the menu. In a small operation, the manager or owner should plan the menu.

The menu should be written several days before it is to be used. Three or four days before serving, there should be a meeting attended by the menu planner, the chef or head cook, the purchasing agent, and the headwaiter or hostess.

The hostess or headwaiter should be asked (1) about any difficulty in serving the items on the menu, then (2) about the popularity of the items as shown by the sales history. If there are serious serving problems, the items causing the difficulties should be eliminated and replaced by other, nonproblem items. Unpopular items which do not sell well should be replaced.

The chef should be asked about any items which are difficult to produce. He should also be asked about the way the work load is balanced among the various stations in his kitchen. Adjustments should be made to improve the balance and to remove troublesome items.

The purchasing department should give information about foods which are difficult to procure for any reason or about those which are unusually high in cost or of poor quality. Changes should be made to replace those items which are unsuitable.

Now the menu should be precosted to make certain that it will produce the desired food cost. If adjustments are needed, they should be made and the menu finalized.

Before food is purchased for this menu and before production begins, a "production sheet" listing the portions of each item to be prepared is made and distributed to purchasing, kitchen, dining rooms, and all other departments concerned. Using the production sheet, purchasing translates quantities to be served into quantities to be purchased and arranges delivery in time for preparation.

Menu planning thus affects purchasing. It is not stating the case too strongly to say that menu planning controls purchasing.

It is at this point that the need for standardized recipes in purchasing becomes apparent. You cannot translate portions to be served into quantities to be purchased without a recipe.

Guessing at quantities results in waste, and waste reduces profit.

Banquet menus require the same careful planning and precosting. A production sheet for banquets must also be made and distributed to all concerned.

Thus, menu planning becomes involved with standardized recipes, customer counts, sales histories, purchasing specifications, buying, storage, and careful receiving. There are, in fact, few areas of restaurant operation which are not affected by menu planning and few which do not affect it.

The problem is to understand all the factors and coordinate them so as to produce a consistently superior product at a consistent profit. This is the function of management.

REVIEW QUESTIONS

1. The purpose of menu planning is to plan a profit. Explain.
2. Who should plan the menu?
3. How is the menu affected by the purchasing department prior to the actual buying of the raw materials?
4. What information must you have to precost a menu?
5. List all the things you must consider while planning your menu.

7.

The Relationship between Menu Planning & Personnel

The menu planner must have a complete knowledge of the skills and abilities of the preparation and service personnel. It would be foolish to place an item on the menu that the cook could not prepare and the waiters could not properly serve. Dishes requiring French service in the dining room would be a mistake if the waitresses were trained only for coffee shop service.

Your menu must be adjusted to the skills of your kitchen and dining room personnel, at least until you can establish standard recipes and standards of service and teach your personnel to use them. Standardized recipes and standards of presentation and service provide the basic tools needed to train and improve your personnel.

You can't install a whole battery of recipes at once, nor can you teach service personnel how to serve every dish overnight. But you can install one perfect dish at a time and teach everyone concerned to serve it perfectly. In a surprisingly short time, you will have a menu made up of very special dishes, served with flair, and each a specialty of your restaurant.

Teaching is a most important function of management. The only way to get the kind of crew you want is to train them. It is most unlikely that you can hire people who already know how to do what you want them to do, even with long experience.

Amateur menu planners can plan your kitchen and dining room into complete confusion and easily defeat the best plans for reducing labor costs. Menu planning requires complete understanding of the problems of producing and serving each menu item.

A skillfully planned menu will balance the work load among the various stations and departments of the kitchen, thus assuring an easy flow of work and quick service. The balanced menu also makes proper preparation and dish-up easier. Good menu planning builds morale; poor menu planning creates dissension.

If you fully understand the problems of service from the standpoint of both the waiter and the customer, you will carefully plan your menu so that it can be served efficiently and graciously within a reasonable length of time. If you do not understand the problems of preparation and service, your menus may easily require more personnel to prepare and serve them than you can afford.

Of course, every menu must be planned for the specific restaurant in which it will be served and for the customers to whom it will be served.

The menu planner must know what you can spend for personnel, also what your particular customers can and will pay. The menu must be planned to satisfy the needs of your customers, and at the same time it must permit preparation and service by personnel whom you can afford in your present kitchen and dining facilities.

REVIEW QUESTIONS

1. Why is it important for a menu planner to know the skills and abilities of all the restaurant's employees?
2. "Teaching is an important function of management." Explain.
3. How does a skillfully planned menu balance the work load in a kitchen?
4. Write a one-week-cycle menu for a college dining room, taking into consideration the fact that they serve three meals a day, seven days a week. The preparation and service personnel are made up for the most part of part-time student help.
5. How can the rise in food and labor costs affect your menu?

The Relation of Menu Planning to Equipment

8.

Every year, thousands of dollars are wasted on unneeded restaurant equipment. Privately owned restaurants are the most common offenders. One rarely opens that is not from 10 to 35 percent overequipped. On the other hand, restaurants opened by franchise operations and successful chains very seldom waste a dime on unneeded equipment. What causes this difference? One thing: planning—especially menu planning.

The chains and the franchisers know what they are going to serve and buy just the equipment needed to produce it. They build the menu before they build the restaurant.

Too many private owners work backwards. They build the restaurant before they plan the menu. They have only a vague idea of what they will serve. How can you buy equipment without knowing what you are going to cook on or in it?

The chains and the franchisers know just what equipment will do the job. They know exactly the raw materials they will use and how they will use them. The private builder usually does not know either of these until he begins to operate, which is too late.

Kitchens and foodservice facilities built by local, state, and federal government agencies are in most cases greatly overequipped. They nearly always have outdated equipment or equipment designed for items no longer produced on the premises of successful restaurants.

If you are planning to build or remodel, take a tour through as many kitchens as you can. And don't go with an equipment salesman! Discuss what you see with the operator. If possible, watch the kitchen work when it is very busy; note any useless gadgets you see, any idle equipment, any wasted space. Also note any equipment which does an exceptional job and reduces the number of necessary personnel.

Now examine your menu and plan your equipment to produce it with a minimum crew in a minimum amount of space. Only after this is done should you consult with an equipment salesman. He should be required to supply fixed prices and to guarantee the delivery and installation date.

Obviously you should not allow a firm who sells equipment to prepare layouts or provide drawings (plans) for your restaurant. Few can resist the temptation to load your restaurant with unneeded but very profitable (for them) pieces of equipment. It should also be apparent that firms who specialize in layout and design are not the best people from whom to buy equipment. Their interest in commissions can sometimes outweigh their obligation to design economically. Be careful about following their recommendations as to where (from which company) to buy. There is frequently a tie-in between designers and equipment houses, the latter giving commissions to designers who bring business to them.

You do the buying—it's your money. Plan your menu, and let it be your guide for buying only what you need. Certainly you need the help of those who are expert in the various aspects of the restaurant business. But be sure you get from them the things you need for your specific problems.

There are many factors that affect the planning of a menu for your new restaurant.

Clientele—who will they be? Where will they come from? What can they spend? What are their needs? How will they come?

Location—will the neighborhood really produce the clientele you are building for? Can you really bring the clientele you want to this location? How? What is the competition? What is the price competition? Is the location convenient for automobiles? For foot traffic?

What will be the business at breakfast? For lunch? At dinner? What will it be on holidays? Weekends?

These are a few of the factors to be considered when you plan your menu for a new restaurant. If you are not opening a new restaurant and must therefore make the best of existing equipment, the problem becomes that of planning the best possible menu to fit this equipment. Obviously you can't feature broiled items without a broiler, nor baked potatoes if there is no oven.

You can plan an interesting, even spectacular menu to fit almost any reasonably equipped kitchen. How good the menu is depends upon your knowledge of food and its preparation and service—and equally, upon what you know about people and what they like to eat.

Plan your specialties and carefully develop recipes and serving instructions. Test them and perfect them one at a time. Then introduce them on your menu. Some will fail, but some will succeed. Keep those which your customers accept. Discard the failures and develop new ones to replace them.

Keep planning, testing, and adding to your menu. Eventually, you will have a customer-accepted menu that is a profit builder and utilizes your equipment to its fullest.

REVIEW QUESTIONS

1. Why is it advisable to plan your menu around your equipment?
2. Plan a coffee shop luncheon menu, taking into consideration that the only equipment they have is (1) deep fat fryer; (2) grill; (3) two-burner cookstove; (4) toaster; (5) coffee urn.
3. List all the equipment needed to prepare the menu on page 41.
4. Who should lay out your kitchen, and what information should you provide him with?
5. What information do you need to determine the location of your restaurant?

9.

STANDARDS:

What Are They?

Why Use Them?

A standard is that which is set up by authority as a rule for the measurement of quantity, quality, weight, measure, or value.

Thus, a standard portion is the exact weight or measure established by management as the portion of a particular product to be served every time.

A standard recipe is a formula established by management to be followed in preparing a product.

A standard of quality is the quality of product acceptable to management.

Standard yield is the number of standard portions which can be produced by a recipe or by a given quantity of meat or other product.

A standard is the criterion by which a product or performance is judged. Good management will set up standards of performance and quality in every area of the restaurant. The comparison of what we do with what we should do (i.e., with the established standard) is the basis for maintaining and improving performance and quality. When improvements are achieved, standards should be adjusted to include them.

Now, what have standards to do with menu planning?

To begin with, you cannot fix cost or set a price unless you have standard portions and standardized recipes. How can you plan a menu without them? A properly planned menu will, if followed, ensure a predetermined profit. You cannot plan a profit unless you know costs. Neither can you set a selling price which will return a profit until you know precisely what your costs will be.

Carefully tested standards effectively enforced will keep costs at a planned level.

Secondly, it is useless to plan a menu unless you have control over quality as well as production. Quality is controlled by carefully established standard recipes, standard purchasing specifications, standard receiving and storage procedures.

The finest food can be ruined by careless, sloppy presentation and by indifferent, unskilled service. It is useless to apply standards of preparation and quality if you do not follow through with effectively enforced standards of presentation and service. Menu planning is intimately concerned with these standards.

You should include instructions for correct presentation (dish-up) and service with each standard recipe. Copies of these instructions should go to those in charge of service in the various rooms.

How do you go about setting up standards?

Standards must be established by a series of tests.

A recipe should be made, taste-tested, adjusted, and made again until it yields a product whose appearance, texture, and flavor are approved. The recipe is then standardized, i.e., it becomes a standard. The quality (flavor, texture, and appearance) also becomes a standard.

If possible, a qualified committee should approve or reject each recipe. In small operations, food and beverage managers with their staff will be responsible. Of course, the chef and/or baker, pastry chef, etc., will be included in the decision-making committee.

Standards of presentation are established by actually dishing up the product with its accompanying garnishes to achieve the best possible presentation . . . then standardizing.

Standard portions are set up by dishing up the product as it will be served, using accepted portion sizes and food costs. It may be desirable to actually serve the food to guests to establish standard portions. Cost should not be a consideration until after the portion is established and standardized. Then, if you cannot afford to serve an acceptable portion at a fair price, drop the whole idea and go to another product.

Standard purchasing specifications are established by examining and testing the products available, then selecting those best suited to your needs and establishing them as standards. Purchasing specifications should specify quality, size, weight or count, trim, etc. There should be a written specification for every product purchased. Those who receive merchandise must have copies of all specifications to ensure that the product received is the same as the product ordered. There is a correct size, quality, shape, and type of product for every recipe. Menu planning is concerned with purchasing specifications because good buying affects both cost and quality of the finished product.

The success or failure of a good operation depends on setting up a *standard of profit* and making it. Many factors besides menu planning enter into establishing a standard of profit, but only a planned menu can ensure a planned profit.

Effective management will set up standards of performance throughout the operation. Standards enable us to compare actual performance and thus continuously provide products and services of dependable high quality. All controls, including food control, wage cost control, liquor control, etc., are achieved by comparing performance with established standards.

REVIEW QUESTIONS

1. What is meant by the term "restaurant standards"?
2. Who determines the standards for a restaurant, and why are they important?
3. "Standards must be established by a series of tests." Explain.
4. How would you set up purchasing standards for a restaurant?
5. In what way are standard portions established?

10.

The Case for Standardized Recipes

The term "standardized recipes" is widely misunderstood. It does not mean that the same recipes are to be used in all restaurants. It does mean reducing your own recipes to your standards and recording them. This makes it possible to produce food equal to your standard of quality time after time.

No one cooking without a recipe can produce exactly the same product day after day. Consequently, the customer may be served a delightful dish once, but when he returns for the same dish, it is not the same. The patron of a good restaurant should be able to return again and again and always receive the same high quality. This can only be done by using a standardized recipe.

The customer is not interested in why the food varies. He wants dependable quality, and it is the management's responsibility to see that he gets it.

There is no way to calculate the cost of a product unless the ingredients and quantities are known. This applies in making shoes or building automobiles. The only way to determine accurate cost is to write down the recipe—a standardized recipe which will be the same every time.

One of the hazards of the restaurant business is the high turnover of chefs and cooks. Restaurants whose reputations depend upon keeping the same chef are subject to his temperament and tantrums. They live in constant fear of his departure and are therefore unable to impose any control over the kitchen, storage, and purchasing departments.

The only way to become independent of the chef and the cook is to standardize the recipes and reduce them to writing. Even a cook with minimal skills can follow a carefully written recipe.

The high rate of turnover among cooks and kitchen personnel makes it necessary to constantly train replacements. Training is difficult and uncertain without written formulas (standardized recipes), but easy and accurate when everything is in writing.

Before quality can be controlled, standards of quality must be established. Unless standards are written down, they will not remain constant. Standards of quality are established by carefully writing down standard recipes and by making certain that the recipes are meticulously followed.

The easy way to get recipes is to copy them out of books. They will not be original or distinctive or different. They will not reflect the individual standards of a distinguished restaurant. There is only one way to get standardized recipes which will make a restaurant distinctive. That is to carefully write down the recipes which make the restaurant successful.

This can't be done by simply asking the chef to write down his recipes. He probably won't do it. And if he does, they probably won't work. Workable, usable recipes can only be had by watching the preparation like a hawk, insisting on weighing and measuring everything and faithfully recording it. The method followed, the times and temperatures—every detail of preparation must become a part of the recipe.

The yield in portions is an essential part of the recipe. Yield cannot be established by dividing the quarts, gallons, or pounds by the size of the portion. The product must be actually dished up under serving conditions to establish yield.

Most restaurant men recognize the need for standardized recipes, but in practice few really use them. As long as they can survive by a system of guesses and approximations, they will not establish and use an effective and accurate control. They will rock along on half the profit they should make rather than take the well-known, established steps necessary to produce the profit to which they are entitled.

Every product needs a formula—even simple processes like boiling eggs for salad, making sandwiches, and so on. No process should be left to guesswork.

REVIEW QUESTIONS

1. Explain the term "standardized recipes."
2. Why are standardized recipes mandatory in precosting a menu?
3. Is it sound business practice to feature a chef's specialty on your menu?
4. What information should be included in a menu production sheet?
5. List the information that should be on a standardized recipe.

II.

How to Set Up and Use Standardized Recipes

If your restaurant is successful, you must have some products which your customers like. Begin with the most popular items. These are the dishes that bring in and hold the business.

Don't start off half-cocked. Plan your procedure—then work your plan.

You can't establish even one standard recipe without the cooperation of your chef and his crew. So talk the plan over with him. Explain the advantages of standardized recipes to you and to him. Assure him that he will have personal copies of all recipes, which he may keep. If you intend making a formula book or a recipe file, give him a copy to keep. All of us like to see our ideas in print; so will he. Tell him how much you need his help, and you'll probably get it.

Don't try to take on the whole job at once; it's too big. So cut it up in pieces, like eating an elephant, and do it a piece at a time. Finish and test each recipe before going on to the next.

Stand beside the chef or cook or *garde-manger* as he prepares the product; weigh, measure, or count every ingredient. Record each process. Check all times with a stop watch.

Now type the recipe. Next, make the product, using the recipe and following it carefully. If it doesn't turn out right, start over again with the chef, and go over each step once more. Then test again until you have the product just the way you want it. Now standardize it and put it into use in the kitchen. Every time the product is made, see that the recipe is followed and that the product really measures up to your standard.

Now you are ready for another product. Proceed as before. Be meticulous and be strict about the standards of flavor, appearance, texture, etc. Do it right!

The recipes you set up will be in fixed quantities. Be sure that you test the yield in portions. Dish them up under serving conditions and actually count the portions. Don't estimate, don't ask anyone, and don't try to figure it out by arithmetic. Test it. Deal in actual yields.

Standard recipes not only ensure consistent quality products; they are your only source of accurate food cost. Now that you know what goes into your products, you can really figure the actual cost. Expect some surprises! The old rule-of-thumb "guesstimates" will look pretty silly compared with your actual costs.

What happens if your standard recipe produces fifty portions, but your sales history shows you need more or less than this number? If you leave it to the kitchen, they will either guess or produce some multiple of fifty orders. If they guess, the product will not be up to standard. If they produce in multiples of fifty, you will have leftovers galore, and either way you will be the loser.

There's a better way. Divide all the quantities of ingredients in your recipe for fifty by 2, and you have a recipe for twenty-five. Divide them by 5, and you have a recipe for ten orders. Divide them by 10, and you have a recipe for five portions. The divided recipe must be prepared and checked for quality and portion size before it is accepted as an equal standard.

Now, if you need thirty-five portions, add the recipe for ten to the recipe for twenty-five. If you need sixty-five portions, add fifty plus ten plus five, and so on.

If your recipe card shows ingredients for fifty in one column, for twenty-five in another, ten in another, and five in another, you or any other normally intelligent person can combine these recipes in such a way as to produce the quantity needed to provide maximum profit. However, before production begins, check to make sure the cook knows what he is doing.

As mentioned earlier, the recipes for various quantities should be made and carefully tested for flavor, appearance, etc.

Preserve in this manner really useful, flexible recipes. Inflexible recipes for fifty to one hundred or any other number are almost completely useless.

AN EXAMPLE OF A STANDARDIZED RECIPE

CHOCOLATE BROWNIES

MATERIALS	WEIGHT
1. Bittersweet chocolate	1 lb.
Butter	1 lb. 8 oz.
Melt chocolate and butter	
2. Eggs	1 lb. 4 oz.
Sugar	3 lb.
Vanilla	1 oz.
Beat until lemon-colored (10 min.)	
Add chocolate to step 2	
3. Cake flour	1 lb.
Sift and fold into mixture	
4. Pecans	1 lb. 8 oz.
Fold into cake mixture and pan up into 18- x 24-in. sheet pans	
Bake at 350 degrees	
Yield: Cut 8 x 24 per sheet pan	

REVIEW QUESTIONS

1. How would you introduce standardized recipes into your daily operation?
2. List all the steps that are necessary in writing a standardized menu.
3. What are you assured of by the use of standardized recipes?
4. Write a standardized recipe for scrambled eggs to feed fifty persons.
5. Write a standardized recipe for a white sheet cake.

How to Conduct and Use Yield Tests to Determine Cost

12.

It is a sad commentary on our industry that most restaurants do not know the cost of a cut of prime rib or a scoop of ice cream or a cup of soup.

True, the large operators—in-plant feeders and successful owner-operated restaurant chains—know their costs; but the great majority of American restaurateurs, even the successful ones, have only a hazy idea of their real costs.

Owners, chefs, and managers will quote off-the-cuff figures; but few can show you written records of actual tests made in their own kitchen. Tests are not difficult to make; and once a reasonable number of tests are accumulated, cost factors can be established which will greatly facilitate costing and pricing of menus.

If you don't know your costs, how can you possibly know your potential profit? How can you fix selling prices without accurate costs?

I know of only one way to determine accurate costs, and that is by conducting your own tests on your own products, in your own kitchen, and under your own serving conditions. Of course, you might hire an expert to run the tests for you; he will be accurate only if he makes the tests under the operating conditions in your restaurant, and hiring his services will cost a great deal more than running the tests yourself.

Don't rely upon costs developed by purveyors or manufacturers. The conditions under which their tests were made will resemble your production and serving conditions only incidentally. Their portion sizes will not necessarily suit your customers. Furthermore, their tendency to base portion costs on arithmetic rather than on actual dish-up invariably produces unrealistic figures which simply do not work out in practice. It's your money being spent, your customers being served, and your profits being lost. So why settle for less than your own tests and your own cost figures?

Dishing up should be done under regular serving conditions, and the entire quantity being tested should be dished at one time to ensure an accurate count. Banquet service offers a good opportunity for such a test. Of course, you need not test 5 gallons. You can make five tests of 1 gallon each, or two tests of 2 1/2 gallons. The combined yield of all the tests will give you figures with which to determine the average cost per portion. The total quantity tested must be sufficient to provide realistic

A SIMPLE TEST RECORD

Brown Derby Restaurant

PRODUCT: Ice Cream **DATE:** October 14

PURVEYOR: ______ **TESTED BY:** J. Smith

		QUANTITY	UNIT COST (AS PURCHASED)	EXTENSION
Vanilla ice cream		5 gal.	$1.95	$9.75
Size of portion:	No. 16 scoop			
Portion yield:	145			
Cost per portion:	$0.0672			
Size of portion:	No. 20 scoop			
Portion yield:	172			
Cost per portion:	$0.0567			

A BUTCHERING, COOKING, AND CARVING TEST

Brown Derby Restaurant

PRODUCT: **Prime Ribs**

PURVEYOR: **Del Monte Meat Co.**

DATE: **October 24**

TESTED BY: **J. Smith**

	QUANTITY, LB.	UNIT PRICE (AS PURCHASED)	EXTENSION
Prime rib, 10-in. trim (as purchased)	280	$0.80	$224.00
Usable raw trim (credit)	63	0.50	(31.50)
	217		192.50
Usable trim and waste	12	N.C.*	N.C.
Trimmed weight (raw)	205	0.94	192.50
Cooked weight	155	1.24	192.50
Bones, fat, and waste	51	N.C.	N.C.
	104	1.85	192.50
Usable cooked trim (credit)	4	0.48	(1.92)
Edible portion	100	1.91	190.58

Size of portion: 10 oz.

Portion yield: 156

Cost per portion: $1.22

(Unaccounted loss: 2 lb. 8 oz.)

* In this example, the restaurant does not give credit for usable trim. In some establishments, a nominal amount of credit is given.

information. Don't base cost figures on a small-quantity test.

A test form like the above (p. 75) may be used for tests of juices, fruits, bulk milk, whipped cream, and similar products which do not involve butchering, cooking, shrinkage, etc.

Note that each step of the butchering, cooking, and carving test (p. 76) must be carefully checked and weighed. The carving must be done under normal carving conditions, and the cooking must be performed under the standard formula in use in your restaurant.

The "cooked weight" has value only as a check against shrinkage. If it varies significantly from your standard, be sure to investigate the quality of meat, cooking temperature, cooking time, etc. (p. 78).

Tests like the preceding three not only give you accurate cost figures for precosting, they also afford a basis for making decisions as to whether or not to buy prefab products.

When a sufficient number of test results to support a valid average cost of the finished product have been accumulated, cost factors may be calculated.

In the case of prime ribs of beef in the second test, the cost of a 10-ounce portion is $1.22. If we divide the cost per portion by the cost per pound as purchased (80 cents), we have a cost factor:

$$1.22 \div 0.80 = 1.525 \qquad \text{cost factor}$$

Thus, you know that the cost of a 10-ounce portion of prime ribs of beef prepared by your own method in your own kitchen by your own people is 1.525 times the cost per pound of 10-inch-trimmed beef ribs.

$$\begin{array}{r} 1.525 \\ \times\ \$0.80 \\ \hline \$1.22000 \end{array}$$

When the price of beef ribs changes, you can simply multiply the new price by 1.525 and find the cost per 10-ounce portion without running tests. In this way, you know before you buy just what the increase or decrease in beef prices will do to your food cost on this particular item.

Make the tests. Accumulate the experience and data. Bring accuracy out of chaos. It can be done easily.

A BUTCHERING TEST

Brown Derby Restaurant — **DATE:** **October 24**

PRODUCT: **Top Sirloin Steak** — **TEST BY:** **J. Smith**

PURVEYOR: **Del Monte Meat Co.**

	QUANTITY	UNIT PRICE (AS PURCHASED)	EXTENSION
Steak block (as purchased)	33 lb.	$1.35	$44.55
Waste and fat	4 lb. 5 oz.	N.C.	N.C.
Usable gross	28 lb. 11 oz.	1.63	44.55
Usable trim (credit)	11 oz.	0.48	(0.33)
Usable for steaks	28 lb.	1.58	44.22
Size of portion: 8 oz.			
Portion yield: 55			
Cost per portion: $0.8040			
(Unaccounted loss: 8 oz.)			

REVIEW QUESTIONS

1. Explain "yield tests."
2. Who should run yield tests, and how should the tests be utilized?
3. On the first test (for ice cream), what would the cost per portion be if you substituted $2.10 in the "unit cost as purchased" column?
4. In the second test, substitute $0.87 for the unit price as purchased, and figure the revised cost per portion.
5. In the third test, substitute $1.75 for the unit price as purchased, and figure the revised cost per portion.

13.

What is a Sales History? Why Keep it?

A sales history is a record of the numbers of each item sold each day. In addition to the single items, it should show the combination of items offered; the price of each; and general information such as serving time, weather, conventions, parades, or other special events which might influence sales.

The menu itself is the best place to record this information. It already incorporates much of the required information. Once you have recorded your sales on it, the menu can be filed under the day of the week, say, Monday, ready to be retrieved when you need it in planning next Monday's menu. In a short time, you will have in your sales history files a number of Monday, Wednesday, and Sunday menus, for example. The days of the week will develop sales patterns of their own. Thus, each day has its own sales history to help you in projecting your sales for next week or next month.

Good sellers will easily be separated from the unpopular items which should be replaced. The accumulated menus will show how each item sells in combination with other items. Thus you will know the sales mix of each menu. This is essential to projecting sales.

Where do you get sales information? Your saleschecks are the best source of sales information. Simply go through the checks and mark each sale after the menu listing of each item. Then total each item in big, easily read figures.

If your restaurant does not use saleschecks, you must carefully record the portions of each item prepared or purchased, then take an actual inventory of the portions left over at the end of the service period. Then record the number of portions of each item actually sold. This process should be repeated after each meal. You may be amazed at the unnecessary leftovers—perhaps, too, at the popular menu items which ran out early. Leftovers and early run-outs are evidence of bad management. They indicate the need for planning.

It is in planning that sales histories have their value. Without this information, you cannot make projections of sales which enable you to accurately precost your menus and to set up sensible production sheets. Unless you can control production, you cannot control either costs or profits. Those who work without sales histories do not deal with facts. Can you afford to have your profits based on uninformed, unfounded estimates?

REVIEW QUESTIONS

1. What is a sales history?
2. Why is it necessary to keep a sales history?
3. Explain the term "sales mix."
4. How do you utilize sales histories in a production sheet?

14.

Precosting: What and Why?

Precosting means determining costs and establishing production quotas before preparation is begun.

It need not be a highly formalized and complicated procedure, as advocated by some consulting firms. The best method is the simplest one which will give you accurate information.

Of course, precosting cannot be done accurately unless you have developed sources of accurate cost figures. These sources are standardized recipes, standardized purchasing specifications, and accurate yield tests.

Production quotas are based upon sales histories. A sales history is a day-by-day record of sales of each menu item. Such a record kept accurately over an extended period is the best basis for projecting sales.

If you don't have these sources of cost and sales information, don't bother with precosting. There is no sense in precosting based upon guesswork.

In the menu on the next page, appetizers and desserts are priced a la carte. The price of the entree includes vegetables, potato, roll, butter, and beverage.

Projected sales, based on past experience as shown by your sales history, are shown by portions under "portions needed." This is the kitchen's guide to production.

The food cost percentages shown are based upon perfect performance, in which every portion prepared is sold. If there are leftovers, the food cost will rise.

If the food cost percentages are too high or too low when compared to your desired percentages, adjustments can be made in selling prices, portions, or items on the menu, while it is still in the planning stage. If the food cost is too low, you may want to replace an entree with a more expensive one, to add better vegetables and/or side dishes, or to include a salad with the entree. If the food cost is too high or too low, corrective measures can be taken before purchasing or production begins and before the menu is printed.

Precosting is an essential part of menu planning. Without it, you cannot plan a profit; neither can you evaluate accurately the package which the customer is expected to buy. The precosting must be compared with actual sales history to have any value at all.

No allowance has been made for employees' meals, which usually average about 2 percent of sales. A more sophisticated projection would figure the cost of food consumed and prepare

PRECOSTING OF A VERY SIMPLE MENU

ITEM	PORTIONS NEEDED	COST EACH	TOTAL COST	SALE PRICE	TOTAL SALES	PERCENTAGE
Seafood Cocktail	41	$0.20	$8.20	$0.75	30.75	
Fruits au Kirsch	15	0.23	3.45	0.65	9.75	
Chicken Gumbo Soup	30	0.07	2.10	0.35	10.50	
Consommé Royal	15	0.06	0.90	0.35	5.25	
TOTAL A LA CARTE APPETIZERS			14.65		56.25	26.04
Pot Roast of Beef	150	0.45	67.50	3.00	450.00	
Fried Chicken	110	0.38	41.80	2.75	302.50	
Baked Ham	100	0.50	50.00	3.25	325.00	
Whipped Potatoes	260	0.02	5.20	—	—	
Candied Yams	150	0.08	12.00	—	—	
Green Beans Amande	360	0.06	21.60	—	—	
Pineapple Rings	100	0.05	5.00	—	—	
Rolls (2) to order	360	0.05	18.00	—	—	
Butter Chips (2)	360	0.03	10.80	—	—	
Coffee	280	0.03	8.40	—	—	
Tea	20	0.02	0.40	—	—	
Milk	60	0.08	4.80	—	—	
TOTAL ENTREES WITH ACCOMPANYING ITEMS			245.50		1,077.50	22.78
Apple Pie (1/5 pie)	100	0.12	12.00	0.40	40.00	
Chocolate Sundae	90	0.16	14.40	0.60	54.00	
TOTAL A LA CARTE DESSERTS			16.40		94.00	17.45
GRAND TOTAL			$276.55		$1,227.75	22.53

sufficient portions to serve the employees. This is an essential part of menu planning.

Too many restaurants work on the theory that they feed the employees on leftovers and, therefore, at no cost. It really costs just as much to serve leftovers as to serve freshly prepared meals to your employees. Besides, if your planning has been carefully done, there will be no leftovers, or at least very few.

Definite meals should be planned and prepared for the employees. The cost of these meals should be included in precosting; the figures will depend on whether you allow your employees to choose from your regular menu, prepare special food for them, or allow them only certain items from the regular menu. Only by making definite plans for employees' meals can you control the cost. When employees are allowed to eat off the regular menu, the added portions needed should be included in the precosting sheet; however, their cost may or may not be considered in the sales price of the finished product, depending on management's policy.

Various types of menus require different precosting practices.

Daily menus, which are written down for each day, must be precosted as they are written. The menu must therefore be written far enough ahead to permit precosting and adjustment.

Cycled menus may be precosted all at one time before the cycle begins. The menu should be precosted again at least every thirty days and whenever there are significant wholesale or retail price changes. As the cycled menus are used, your sales history will reflect a sales mix, which will affect your precosting results when applied to your menus.

New items should be precosted before they are placed on the menu.

Restaurants which use a fixed menu (the same every day) should precost the menu at least every thirty days and whenever there are price changes at wholesale or retail.

Banquet menus should be precosted before they are offered for sale, and again every thirty days and whenever wholesale or retail prices change.

No matter how simple or how complex your operation is, you cannot realize maximum profits or plan menus intelligently without precosting.

REVIEW QUESTIONS

1. What is precosting?
2. Where would you find the information needed to do a precosting sheet?
3. How would you use a precosting sheet in your restaurant operation?
4. How could you reduce your food cost percentages by utilizing a precosting sheet?

15. The Production Sheet: What is It? Why Use It?

DAILY PRODUCTION SHEET

RESTAURANT________ TIME________ DATE OF SERVICE________

Item	Size of Portion	Portions to Prepare	Total Amounts to Prepare	Formula No.
Chicken Noodle Soup	8-oz. ladle	100	6⅔ gal.	1006
Braised Beef Stew	8-oz. ladle	120	10 gal.	1612
Filet of Sole	5 oz.	60	20 lb.	1881
French Fried Potatoes	3 oz. cooked	60	15 lb. frozen	931
Green Peas with Onions	3 oz. cooked	60	12 lb. frozen	912
Pumpkin Pie	⅕ pie	30	6 pies	103
Coffee	2 cups	120	12 gal.	293

The production sheet (as the example on p. 92 shows) is an instruction to your kitchen and purchasing department to buy and prepare certain foods in certain quantities, to be served at a specific time in a specific place. Without a production sheet of some sort, there can be no control over production or purchasing, which means no intelligent control over food cost.

There is little purpose in fixing prices, planning portions, establishing standardized recipes, precosting menus, or testing for costs unless you also control production. Overproduction and overbuying are the chief causes of high food costs.

Every item on the menu must appear on the production sheet, which must include:

1. The quantity of each item to be prepared (expressed both in portions and in units of weight or measure)
2. Size of portion
3. When and where food is to be served

Of course, there must be separate production sheets for each meal and for each special service, such as banquets, receptions, luncheons, catering services, etc.

Items to be served for employees' meals must also be listed with quantities to prepare. These may be added to your regular production sheets or shown on a separate sheet—they must not be ignored. Don't let employees' meals become a chef's or cook's alibi for overproduction.

The most difficult part of setting up a production sheet is determining how much to purchase and/or prepare. There is no infallible guide to projecting sales. No one can predict them 100 percent.

The best-known method is to base your estimates of quantities needed on your past experience, using carefully kept sales histories to reveal past sales experience. By using them and allowing for events, conditions, weather, etc. which may affect sales, you can project reasonably accurate sales figures on which to base each day's preparation.

You must have the courage to prepare just what you need and the courage to run out if you make a poor projection—plus the resourcefulness to substitute for the items which run out.

It is questionable if you can afford to serve leftovers anyway. By the time you reinvest labor to make them over, they are too expensive to sell at the reduced prices leftovers bring.

In a city restaurant, where there are dependable daily deliveries, the iceboxes should be empty at the end of the day, except for items which must be preprepared for tomorrow's menus. Storerooms too should contain only the quantities needed for immediate use.

Such controls are possible only if planning is done far enough in advance to permit purchasing and prepreparation of exact quantities needed. This means the menus must be planned, the costs determined, the prices set, the quantities projected, the formulas ready, and the production sheets completed at least three days before production begins.

Sounds complicated, doesn't it? It is, and it will be unless you establish procedures which will produce the needed information without confusion and on time.

Even if you serve the same menu every day, you need a production sheet every day. True, it is easier not to prepare it, but it is vitally important.

If you serve a cycled menu, you need a daily production sheet based on the specific menu needs of each day.

No operation is so simple or so complex that it can do without a production estimate every day. Besides wasting food, overproduction wastes preparation labor, the most expensive cost. It wastes storage facilities, refrigerator space, and freezer space. There really is nothing to be gained by buying, storing, and preparing food that you do not need and cannot sell.

To survive, restaurants must learn to eliminate all waste of every kind. The only way to do this is to plan. The "production sheet" is a valuable tool; it correlates planning with production and production with sales, and it eliminates waste.

But, like all good tools, it cannot help you if you don't use it. No plan or system will work by itself. Good management is necessary to make the system function and achieve results.

REVIEW QUESTIONS

1. What is a kitchen production sheet?
2. Who makes out the kitchen production sheet, and how does it affect production?
3. When should a kitchen production sheet be made out?
4. What information must be included on a kitchen production sheet?
5. How do leftovers fit into a kitchen production sheet?

16.

How to Determine the Selling Price

"To determine the selling price, multiply the cost of the food by 3" (or 4, or 2 1/2).

"To find the selling price, multiply the cost of the meat by 5."

Sadly enough, these are axioms of the restaurant business. Of course, they are ridiculous, just as pricing shoes at six times the cost of rubber heels would be ridiculous.

It should be evident to all that the selling price must be sufficient to pay all costs and still provide a reasonable profit. It follows that you must know all the costs, every one of them, before you can fix a selling price. Profit must be added to the combined expenses and the price adjusted to provide a predetermined profit, after all expenses are paid.

Thus, profit is treated as an expense and provided for just as other expenses are provided for. If you don't plan a profit, the chances of making one are very poor indeed.

Assume that these figures are all the expenses of an operation except cost of food sold and that the sales are $15,000 per month:

FIGURE 1

Cost of food sold		
Wages and salaries	$5,610.00	37.4%
Employees' meals	300.00	2.0
Payroll taxes and employee welfare	375.00	2.5
Fuel	300.00	2.0
Lights and power	120.00	0.8
China and glassware	75.00	0.5
Silverware	75.00	0.5
Utensils	45.00	0.3
Paper supplies	60.00	0.4
Linens	120.00	0.8
Uniforms	135.00	0.9
Menus	35.00	0.2
Accounting	525.00	3.5
Miscellaneous	75.00	0.5
Repairs and maintenance	270.00	1.8
Rent	720.00	4.8
Depreciation	915.00	6.1
Outside signs	105.00	0.7
Cleaning supplies	105.00	0.7
Window washing and janitor	150.00	1.0
Expenses before profit	$10,110.00	67.4%
Profit	750.00	5.0
Total expenses	$10,860.00	72.4%

All expenses except "cost of food sold" are known. These expenses total 67.4 percent of the gross sales. What must the food cost be in order to provide a 5 percent profit?

FIGURE 2

ADD:	67.4%	Expenses
	+ 5.0%	
	72.4%	Expenses and profit
SUBTRACT:	100.0%	
	− 72.4%	
	27.6%	Food cost
If you prefer to work with dollars:		
ADD:	$10,110	Expenses
	+ 750	Profit
	$10,869	Expenses and profit
SUBTRACT:	$15,000	Gross sales
	− 10,860	Expenses and profit
	$ 4,140	Allowable cost of food sold
	27.6%	
	15 /4,140.00	Allowable cost of food sold

The desired percentage of the selling price (and this will give you food cost) is 27.6. If you exceed this cost, you decrease profit. That is the only place where you can get money to pay excess food cost.

To set a sales price that will produce a 27.6 percent food cost, divide cost of food by 27.6 percent. The answer is 1 percent of the sales price. Multiply by 100, and this is the sales price.

FIGURE 3

	1% of selling price
Desired percent	/cost of food
1% of sales price × 100 = sales price	

This does not mean that every item must yield a 27.6 percent food cost. It does mean that all items sold must produce a net food cost of 27.6 percent of sales.

An order of macaroni and cheese which cost $0.0936 might be sold for 65 cents at a 14.2 percent food cost and still be a good value to your customers. An order of roast beef costing $0.9302 would need to be sold at $3.40 to return a 27.6 percent food cost. It could be necessary to reduce the selling price to $2.75 in order to attract a reasonable number of sales. At $2.75, the food cost becomes 33.8 percent.

To have customer acceptance, various items must be sold at various food cost percentages. Low- and high-food cost items must be combined on the menu because of what the customer will pay for each item. The result is a balanced menu which produces the desired food cost. When the ratio of sales (sales mix) is known, the combined food cost percentage for all the menu items can be calculated in advance to ensure that the selling prices are sufficent to provide for both expenses and profit.

We plan a menu to yield a certain profit. We then compare the actual results with the planned results, making corrections and adjustments to bring actual performance into line with planned performance. By comparing what we "did do" with what we "should do," day by day, we are able to make adjustments that ensure a planned profit (see unit on precosting).

The foregoing tends to emphasize the importance of costs and cost control. It has long been a fault of the restaurant industry to apply too much effort to controlling costs and too little effort to merchandising and sales promotion.

We cannot "charge what the market will bear, and forget costs," as some have suggested. But we can adjust our prices according to what the customer will pay within the limitations necessary to produce an acceptable profit.

A well-planned menu will contain items which provide a high percentage of profit as well as those which provide a low percentage of profit. They must be skillfully balanced to provide the desired amount of profit.

FIGURE 4

		Price, $	Percentage
A. Spaghetti Tetrazzini			
	Selling price	0.80	100
	Cost of food	0.16	20
	Gross profit	0.64	80
B. Top Sirloin Steak Maitre d'Hotel			
	Selling price	3.00	100
	Cost of food	1.20	40
	Gross profit	1.80	60

It is important to remember that we do not operate a business to make percentages, but rather to make dollars.

Consider the cases shown in Figure 4:

Item A provides a gross profit of 80 percent, which equals 64 cents.

Item B provides only 60 percent gross profit but leaves $1.80 with which to pay bills and provide profit.

Items with a higher selling price can be sold at a higher-percentage food cost and still yield more dollars of profit. Usually the higher the check average, the greater the dollar profit from each sale. Sales volume also enters into the production of profit.

The restaurant in Figure 1 makes a profit of 5 percent on $15,000 of sales per month. The cost of food sold is $4,140, which is 27.6 percent of sales.

If, by good merchandising, advertising, and careful attention to the quality of the food and service, we are able to increase sales by 10 percent, total sales will then be $16,500. The cost of food will still be 27.6 percent, or $4,554—an increase of only $414.

It should not be necessary to increase labor to handle this 10 percent increase in sales, but of course rent, accounting, depreciation, outside signs, janitorial expense, and similar costs in laundry, uniforms, linens, etc. are directly related to sales volume. These expenses total $1,035, so if they increase by 10 percent, it amounts to $103.50.

Out of the added $1,500 sales, we must pay $414 for food sold and $103.50 for expenses, leaving $982.50 extra profit. This increases the profit from $750 to $1,732.50 and increases the percentage of profit from 5 percent to 10.5 percent.

The 10 percent increase in sales more than doubled the profit. There is a lesson here somewhere. . . . a 10 percent increase in sales will add more to your profit than saving 20 percent of your food cost. Go after increased volume—you'll never *save* yourself rich!

A word about the loss leader myth: In a drugstore or supermarket, a customer walks past several thousand articles in order to buy the loss leader. Usually he buys several other items. In a restaurant, however, the customer comes in and buys your loss leader and walks out. He very seldom buys another meal at the regular price on the way out. So loss leaders are not for restaurants.

Nevertheless, skillfully planned discount sales are effective and profitable sales builders and good merchandising gimmicks. There are a few rules to follow:

1. Choose a low-cost, long-profit item for your discount sale. In this way, you can make a dramatic price reduction and still retain a satisfactory profit margin.
2. Choose a well-known item which is a popular seller in your restaurant and discount it.
3. The food cost at discount should be at or below your desired food cost.
4. When the sale is over, go back to your regular price, just as a clothing store does.

Merchandising by combinations also has several advantages:

	Cost	Retail
Ham Sandwich	$0.15	$0.65
Jellied Fruit Salad	0.05	0.30
Pie	0.06	0.30
	$0.26	$1.25

These three long-profit items have a combined food cost of 20.8 percent. If the price is cut to 99 cents, the food cost will be 26.3 percent. This 25-cent discount is a dramatic price reduction and attractive to your customers, yet it still leaves you with a satisfactory margin of profit.

There is not a good reason to include coffee or other beverage in the combinations whose discounted price is higher than your present check average.

There is no sense in merchandising items which will not provide a reasonable profit. If you increase the sale of such an item one hundredfold, you will not increase your profit at all. One hundred times zero equals zero.

REVIEW QUESTIONS

1. How do you determine the selling price of a menu item?
2. Using the percentage figure on page 99, determine the

selling price of a New York strip sirloin steak if the raw food cost is $1.10.

3. Should all menu items in a restaurant have the same percentage of markup?
4. "It is important to remember that we do not operate a business to make percentages, but rather to make dollars." Explain.
5. What is a loss leader?

MENU SUGGESTIONS 17.

This section contains a list of menu suggestions that can be utilized in planning menus. Every menu planner should make his own list of menu items, based on the eating habits of the public to which he is catering and arranged for quick and easy reference. New ideas should be added to the list as industry introduces new products.

Most fast-food operations and many of the better restaurants are using convenience foods to hold down increasing labor costs and to improve their menus with a wide variety of food selections that have been tested nationally and accepted by the eating public. Food costs in recent years have also risen, and the institution feeder has been forced to introduce soy protein solids into his menu in the form of meat substitutes or extenders.

The first requisite in menu planning is to know for whom the menu is planned and what they like to eat. Variety in menus is important; also the quality and quantity of the food, its appearance, its flavor, and its nutritional factors. Garnishes not only should have eye appeal and make a picture but should be edible. Garnishes must be dainty.

BREAKFAST

Appetizers

Orange Juice
Grapefruit Juice
Tomato Juice
Pineapple Juice
Cherry Juice Cocktail
Fresh Rhubarb and Strawberry Juice Cocktail
Fresh Vegetable Juice Cocktail
Mango Juice
Fresh Cherry Juice
Fresh Cranberry Juice Cocktail

Fruits

Fresh Fruit Cocktail—oranges, peaches, pears, pineapple, plums, raspberries, strawberries, figs, cherries, apricots
Fresh Pineapple Cocktail

Fresh Grapefruit and Orange Cup
Fresh Melon—Honeydew, Casaba, Watermelon
Fresh Papaya
Grapefruit
Bananas
Royal Anne Cherries
Apples, Mangoes
Apricot Halves
Citrus Fruit Cup

Cooked Fruits

Stewed Apple Slices
Stewed Apricots
Stewed Fruit Compote
Stewed Prunes
Baked Bananas
Baked Rhubarb
Stewed Fresh or Dry Peaches
Baked Pears, Spiced
Figs

Entrees

Omelet
Fluffy Omelet
Bacon Omelet
Cheese Omelet
Chicken Liver Omelet
Ham Omelet
Lobster Omelet
Boiled Eggs
Soft-boiled Eggs
Fried Eggs
Mushroom Omelet
Jelly Omelet
Western Omelet
Poached Egg on Toast
Poached Egg on Toast with Asparagus au Gratin
Poached Egg Grand Duc
Poached Egg with Corned Beef

Poached Egg Parmentier
Poached Eggs Mornay
Eggs Benedict
Poached Eggs with Hollandaise Sauce
Scrambled Eggs with Cheddar Cheese
Scrambled Eggs with Chipped Beef
Scrambled Eggs with Chopped Bacon
Scrambled Eggs with Chopped Chicken Liver and Bacon
Scrambled Eggs with Fine Herbs
Scrambled Eggs with Chopped Ham
Scrambled Eggs with Mushrooms
Scrambled Eggs with Tomatoes
Scrambled Eggs with Chopped Green Chilies
Baked Eggs (Shirred Eggs)
Shirred Eggs au Gratin
Shirred Eggs Creole
Shirred Eggs with Bacon
Shirred Eggs with Chicken Liver
Shirred Eggs with Creamed Chicken
Shirred Eggs with Lobster
Shirred Eggs with Sausage
Fried Liver and Bacon
Brains Scrambled with Eggs
Broiled Brains
Braised Kidneys
Baked Ham
Bacon and Mushrooms Grilled on Toast
Grilled Sausage Patties
Sausage and Chips
Fried Calf's Brains
Grilled Calf's Liver and Bacon
Fried Chicken Livers and Bacon on Toast
Fried Fish and Chips
Vegetable Cutlets
Banana Fritters with Raspberry Sauce
Corn Fritters
Asparagus Rarebit on Toast
Plain Pancakes
Thin Cream Pancakes
Deluxe Fresh Buttermilk Pancakes
French Pancakes
Swedish Pancakes

Buckwheat Pancakes
Rice Pancakes
Creamed Chicken Pancakes
Creamed Tuna Pancakes
Almond Pancakes
Apple Pancakes
Banana Pancakes
Blackberry Pancakes
Chili Pancakes
Chocolate Pancakes
Coconut Pancakes
Corn Pancakes
Ham Pancakes
Pineapple Pancakes
Raspberry Pancakes
Sausage Pancakes
Strawberry Pancakes
Raisin Waffles
Blueberry Waffles
Corn Waffles
Ham Waffles

Toast

White Bread
Rolls
Cinnamon Bun
Cinnamon Bread
Doughnuts
English Muffins
French Toast
Milk Bread
Fruit Bread
Whole Wheat Bread
Salt Rising Bread
Bran Muffins
Plain Muffins
Hush Puppies
Apple Cake
Peach Cake
Jelly Doughnuts

Raised Doughnuts
Cake Doughnuts
Chocolate Doughnuts
Oatmeal Cookies
Molasses Cookies
Lemon Wafers
Spongecake Cookies
Melba Toast
Pecan Rolls
Hot Biscuits
Coffee Cake
Corn Pones
Popovers
Crullers

Coffee Cakes

Almond Cake
Cinnamon Cake
Dutch Apple Cake
Fruit Cake
Prune-filled Cake
Swedish Cardamon Cake
Orange Cake
Raisin Cake
Coffee Ring
Danish Pastries

Sweet Rolls

Caramel Rolls
Cinnamon Buns
Currant Buns
Hot Cross Buns
Orange Sweet Rolls
Pecan Sweet Rolls
Prune Sweet Rolls
Raisin Twist Sweet Rolls

LUNCH

Appetizers

Fruit Cocktail
Fresh Pineapple Cocktail
Half Grapefruit
Fresh Grapefruit Supreme
Fresh Fruit Cup
Grapefruit and Avocado Cocktail
Orange and Avocado Cocktail
Melon Cocktail
Melon and Raspberry Cocktail
Fresh Pineapple and Raspberry Cocktail
Orange and Raspberry Cocktail
Clam Juice Cocktail
Fresh Cherry Juice Cocktail
Fresh Rhubarb and Strawberry Juice
Fresh Orange Juice
Fresh Grapefruit Juice
Tomato Juice Cocktail
Fresh Cranberry Juice Cocktail
Fresh Vegetable Juice Cocktail
Mixed Seafood Cocktail
Oysters on the Half Shell
Shrimp Cocktail
Deviled Crabmeat Cocktail
Deviled Lobster Cocktail
Fresh Crabmeat Cocktail
Fresh Lobster Cocktail
Clams on the Half Shell
Marinated Salmon in Aspic
Fresh Shrimp in Aspic
Deviled Egg and Olive
Antipasto
Smorgasbord
Relish Tray
Stuffed Celery
Stuffed Celery with Anchovies
Celery Curls

Celery Hearts
Piccalilli
Bengal Club Chutney
Beet Relish
Corn Relish
Spiced Watermelon Pickle
Pickled Cauliflower
Bhajia (Potato Fritters)
Onion Fritters
Spiced Crabapples
Spiced Peaches
Spiced Apricots
Spiced Cherries
Spiced Mangoes
Spiced Prunes
Cottage Cheese and Chives
Cottage Chees and Olives
Crabmeat Canapé
Lobster Canapé
Tuna Fish Canapé
Liver Sausage Canapé
Chopped Chicken Liver Canapé
Caviar
Smoked Salmon Canapé
Ham Canapé
Chicken Canapé
Tongue Canapé
Salami Canapé
Shrimp Canapé
Salmon and Caviar Canapé
Crabflake Balls
Chopped Beef Liver
Sardine Vinaigrette
Deviled Sardine Canapé
Crabmeat Canapé Parmesan
Cheese Cookie Canapé
Cheese Sticks
Cheese Fritters
Canapé Roquefort
Oysters Casino
Oyster Canapé
Deviled Oysters

Soups

Alphabet Soup
Chicken Noodle Soup
Chicken Rice Soup
Chicken Mulligatawny
Corn Chowder
Corn and Tomato Chowder
Creole Chicken Gumbo
Creole Chowder
Imperial Chicken Soup
Old Plantation Soup
Swiss Potato Soup
Beef Barley Soup
Borsch
English Beef Soup
French Onion Soup
Fresh Vegetable Soup
Minestrone
Oxtail Soup
Tomato Bouillon
Tomato Soup (Homemade)
Tomato Noodle Soup
Tomato Soup with Rice
Chicken Consommé
Jellied Chicken Consommé
Consommé
Consommé Julienne
Consommé Vermicelli
Consommé with Noodles
Consommé with Rice
Clam Broth
Coney Island Clam Chowder
Manhattan Clam Chowder
Crab Chowder
Crab Soup
Jellied Tomato Bouillon
Mock Turtle Soup
Scotch Barley Broth
Philadelphia Pepper Pot
Boston Clam Chowder
Cape Cod Clam Chowder

New England Clam Chowder
Cheese Soup
Cream of Cheese Soup
Clam Bisque
Crab Bisque
Oyster Bisque
Lobster Bisque
Cream of Carrot Soup
Cream of Cauliflower Soup
Cream of Celery Soup
Cream of Chicken Soup
Cream of Corn Soup
Cream of Fresh Asparagus Soup
Cream of Mushroom Soup
Cream of Pea Soup
Cream of Potato Soup
Purée Jackson
Cream of Tomato Soup
Tomato Bisque
Cream of Fresh Watercress Soup
Cream of Fresh Spinach Soup
Vichyssoise (Cold Cream of Potato Soup)
Black Bean Soup
Lentil Soup
Navy Bean Soup
Purée Mongole
Split Pea Soup
Mutton Soup
Lamb Soup
Turkey Soup
Duck Soup

Entrees: Beef

Cubed Steak
Cheddar Steak
Talk of the Town Steak
Braised Beef Steak Smothered in Onions
Steak Country Style
Steak Inverness
Spanish Steak

Pepper Steak
Grilled Ground Beef
Chopped Sirloin Steak
Tenderloin Steak
Filet Mignon
Chateaubriand
Beef Bourguignonne
Steak Tartare (Raw Lean Ground Beef)
Braised Tenderloin Slices
Beef Stroganoff—Steamed Rice
Russian Réchauffé
Tenderloin Steak en Brochette
Pepper Steak Espagnole
Chopped Tenderloin Steak
Tenderloin Steak Pot Pie
Roast Prime Ribs of Beef
Hot Prime Rib Sandwich
Roast Whole Round of Beef (Bone In)
Roast Round of Beef (Boneless)
French Dip Sandwich
Roast Sirloin of Beef
Roast Crossrib of Beef
Roast Brisket of Beef
Hot Roast Beef Sandwich
Roast Beef Hash
Braised Diced Beef and Onions
Braised Short Ribs of Beef
Browned Beef Stew
Individual Beef Steak Hot Pie
Braised Sirloin Steak Tips
Braised Pot Roast of Beef
Pot Roast Hash
Braised Beef with Garden Vegetables
Potted Swiss Steak
Swedish Meatballs
Hungarian Goulash with Noodles
Viennese Beef Goulash
Roulade of Beef
Spanish Beef Stew
Salisbury Meat Loaf
Braised Beef and Noodles
Hamburger

Cheeseburger
Chili Burger
Meat Loaf with Mushroom Gravy
Baked Meat Balls with Rice
Chopped Beef and Noodles
Chopped Beef and Macaroni
Ground Beef Stew with Curry Dumplings
Stuffed Bell Peppers
Barbecued Beef on a Bun
Beef Hash, Country Style
Manhattan Steak
Fried Beef and Cabbage
Beef Croquettes
Beef and Noodle Casserole
Boiled Beef Flanken
Boiled Beef with Horseradish Sauce
Corned Beef and Cabbage
Corned Beef Hash
Corned Beef Hash with Fried Eggs
Corned Beef and Spaghetti Casserole
Corned Beef and Rice Casserole
Corned Beef and Noodle Casserole
Pepper Stuffed with Corned Beef
Boiled Beef with Sauerkraut
New England Boiled Dinner
London Broil
Stuffed Flank Steak
Jellied Beef Tongue
Boiled Beef Tongue
Frankfurter and Green Bean Casserole
Pigs in a Basket
Barbecued Frankfurters
Frank and Hot Potato Salad
Frankfurters and Sauerkraut
Frankfurter and Macaroni Loaf
Frankfurters and Beans
Fried Beef Liver and Bacon
Smothered Liver and Onions
Baked Yearling Liver with Bacon
Glazed Lucheon Meat
Grilled Luncheon Meat
Luncheonburger

Tripe Sauté
Tripe with Spanish Sausage
Honeycomb Tripe Creole
Brains Scrambled with Eggs
Braised Kidney
Beef Steak and Kidney Pie
Kidney Creole
Baked Stuffed Heart
Beef Heart Pot Roast
Macaroni and Cheese with Chipped Beef
Creamed Chipped Beef
Braised Beef Joint
Oxtail Ragout
Beef Kebab
Shish Kebab
Spaghetti and Meatballs
Ravioli
Beef Chow Mein
Beef Chop Suey
Beef Mandarin

Lamb

Roast Leg of Lamb
Broiled Lamb Stew
Barbecued Lamb Steak
Broiled Lamb Rib Chops
Roast Lamb Loin
Broiled Lamb Chop with Kidney
Crown Roast of Lamb
Lamb Chop Mixed Grill
Baked Lamb and Lima Beans
Irish Lamb Stew
Browned Lamb Stew
Braised Lamb with Vegetables
Roast Shoulder of Lamb with Dressing
Shoulder Chop Imperial
Braised Lamb Shanks
Braised Breast of Lamb
Grilled Lamb Patty with Bacon
Lamb Hot Pot

Curried Lamb
Shepherd's Pie
Lamb Croquettes
Mutton Biriyani
Mutton Curry
Mutton Cutlets

Pork

Pork Chop Sauté
Breaded Pork Chops
Breaded Pork Cutlets
Baked Stuffed Pork Chops with Rice and Tomatoes
Creole Pork Chop
Barbecued Pork Chop
Baked Pork Chops and Noodles
Baked Pork Chops and Apples
Honey-glazed Pork Chop
Baked Ham (Canned)
Baked Ham Virginia Style (Smoked Ham)
Baked Ham Steak
Cold Baked Ham
Hot Baked Ham Sandwich
Boiled Ham and Cabbage
Diced Ham and Lima Beans
Roast Leg of Pork
Roast Loin of Pork
Hot Pork Sandwich
Grilled Ham Steak
Ham Steak Montmorency
Ham Steak Hawaiian
Ham Steak with Pineapple
Glazed Ham Patties
Grilled Chopped Ham Steak
Breaded Pork Cutlets (Boneless)
Breaded Stuffed Pork Bird
Georgia Brunswick Pork Stew
Pork Curry
Creole Pork Casserole
Spanish Pork and Noodles
Pork Soufflé

Baked Pork Hash, Country Style
Braised Pork Stew
Baked Ham and Macaroni
Ham Fritters
Ham Puffs
Ham a la King—Hot Biscuits
Ham and Noodle au Gratin
Ham Croquettes
Scalloped Potatoes and Ham
Ham Loaf with Fruit Sauce
Ham and Macaroni Creole
Barbecued Ham Sandwich
Scalloped Ham and Cabbage
Casserole of Ham and Peas
Barbecued Spareribs
Baked Spareribs and Dressing
Baked Spareribs with Sauerkraut
Boiled Spareribs with Sauerkraut
Black-eyed Peas, Rice and Bacon Square (Hopping John)
Baked Bean and Bacon Square
Breaded Pork Tenderloin
Roast Suckling Pig
Pork Tamale Pie
Pork Chow Mein
Pork Chop Suey

Veal

Roast Leg of Veal
Roast Loin of Veal
Smothered Veal T-bone Steak
Veal T-bone with Bacon Strip
Baked Veal Chops
Veal Cutlets Cordon Bleu
Cutlet Vienna
Breaded Veal Cutlets
Veal Cutlets Baked in Tomato Sauce
Veal Cutlets with Mushroom and Spaghetti
Veal Cutlet Holstein
Veal Cutlet Baked in Milk
Veal Cutlet Hungarian

Chopped Veal and Sausage Patty
Baked Veal Loaf
Grilled Veal Patty with Bacon
Veal Rosettes
Veal Stew
Veal Fricassee
Veal Paprika
Veal Casserole with Rice
Veal Ragout
Veal Goulash
Braised Veal and Noodles
Baked Veal Shoulder
Braised Breast of Veal
Creamed Calf's Brain
Veal Kidney Stew
Braised Veal Kidneys
Grilled Calf's Liver and Bacon
Veal a la king

Poultry

Chicken Pot Pie
Chicken Fricassee with Biscuits
Chicken Stew with Dumplings
Smothered Chicken with Mushrooms
Braised Chicken
Chicken Brunswick Stew
Batter-fried Chicken
Baked Egg Noodles and Chicken
Baked Chicken au Gratin
Country Fried Chicken
Maryland Fried Chicken
Fried Chicken Chasseur
Southern Fried Chicken
Butter-baked Chicken Breast
Breast of Chicken and Fried Ham
Breast of Chicken Supreme
Hickory-broiled Chicken
Charcoal-broiled Chicken
Mahogany-broiled Chicken
Thanthurry Spiced Chicken

Broiled Chicken
Roast Chicken
Baked Chicken and Wild Rice
Fowl in Foil
Chicken Paprika
Barbecued Chicken
Baked Chicken
Savory Baked Chicken
Chicken Leg Pot Pie
Chicken Curry
Breaded Chicken Leg
Chicken Cutlets
Fricassee of Chicken Wings
Chicken Amandine
Chicken Divan
Creamed Chicken with Mushrooms
Chicken Croquettes
Baked Chicken Loaf
Chicken Fritters
Barbecued Chicken on a Bun
Chicken a la King on Toast
Jellied Chicken
Chicken Timbale with Cream Gravy
Chicken Biriyani
Chicken Cacciatore
Hot Chicken Tamale
Chicken Taco Meat
Chicken Chop Suey
Fried Rice with Chicken
Chicken Vindalo
Chicken Kiev
Chicken Livers with Chicken Gravy
Chicken Livers with Mushroom Patty
Creole Giblets
Creamed Chicken Giblets
Sautéed Giblets with Steamed Rice
Roast Turkey
Corn Bread Dressing
Baked Turkey Loaf
Braised Turkey Wing
Baked Turkey Hash (Country Style)
Turkey Croquettes

Hot Turkey Sandwich
Turkey Goulash
Sliced Turkey Sandwich
Baked Noodles and Turkey
Roast Capon
Roast Duck
Braised Duck
Duck Stew

Fish

Baked Fillet of Cod
Baked Salmon Steak
Baked Mackerel
Baked Breaded Fillet of Haddock
Baked Stuffed Fillet of Blue Pike
Deep-fat-fried Blue Pike
Deep-fat-fried King Whiting
Fisherman's Platter
Mixed Sea Food Platter
Seafood Newburg
Lobster Newburg
Shrimp Newburg
Crabmeat Newburg
Scallop Newburg
Oyster Newburg
Fresh Crabmeat Louisiana
Fresh Shrimp Louisiana
Creole Salmon
Poached Codfish
Poached Haddock
Creamed Pollack
Creamed Shrimp
Creamed Flounder
Fish Cake with Golden Sauce
Welsh Rarebit Scrod
Codfish Cake
Salmon Patties
Salmon Croquettes
Tuna Fish Loaf
Salmon Loaf

Gefilte Fish
Broiled Brook Trout
New England Salt Fish Dinner
Steamed Finnan Haddie
Fillet of Sole
Fillet of Sole Marguery
Stuffed Flounder
Planked Individual Flounder
Frogs' Legs Sauté
Grilled Halibut Steak
Broiled Salt Mackerel
Baked Stuffed Salmon
Grilled Fillet of Sea Bass
Broiled Shad Roe with Bacon
Fried Smelts
Smoked Whitefish
Cherrystone Clam Stew
Fried Clams
Clam Fritters
Steamed Clams
Roast Clams
Steamed Crabs
Crab Cakes Imperial
Deviled Crab
Baked Crabmeat and Oysters on Toast
Seafood a la Home
Soft Shell Crab Sauté
Fried Soft Shell Crabs
Broiled Lobster
Boiled Lobster
Lobster Thermidor
Broiled Lobster Tails
Oyster Stew
Fried Oysters
Oysters Longchamp
Oysters Rockefeller
Oysters Casino
Baked Oysters Lafayette
Oyster Crumb Broil
Scalloped Oysters
Creamed Oysters
Broiled Oysters

Broiled Oysters with Bacon
Grilled Oysters and Bacon, Southern Style
Panned Oysters
Broiled Scallops and Bacon en Brochette
Fried Deep-sea Scallops
Boiled Shrimp
Steamed Shrimp
French-fried Shrimp
Shrimp Meunière on Rice Nest
Shrimp Curry with Rice
Shrimp Saki
Shrimp Scampi
Boiled Terrapin
Fried Turtle Cutlet
Turtle Curry with Rice

Eggs, Cheese

Asparagus Rarebit on Toast
Baked Noodles and Tomatoes au Gratin
Cheese and Noodle Loaf with Creole Sauce
Macaroni au Gratin
Noodle, Cheese, Tomato, and Bacon Scallop
Spaghetti and Tomatoes au Gratin
Tuna and Noodle Loaf with Cream Sauce
Baked Polenta with Cheese
Cheese Cutlets
Cheese Fondue on Toast
Stuffed Green Peppers, Spanish Style
Green Peppers Stuffed with Minced Meat
Fresh Creamed Asparagus on Toast
Vegetable Plate with Poached Eggs
Vegetable Cutlets
Fried Rice with Mixed Vegetables
Egg Cutlets

Vegetables

Boiled Artichokes
Artichokes au gratin
Artichokes Sauté

Boiled Jerusalem Artichokes
Buttered Asparagus
Creamed Asparagus
Buttered Asparagus Spears
Asparagus Tips au Gratin
Baked Chick Peas
Garbanzo Beans, Southern Style
Honey-baked Chick Peas
Marinated Chick Peas
Puréed Chick Peas
Kidney Beans in Red Wine
Mexican Kidney Beans
Spanish Kidney Beans
Pink Beans with Herbs
Red Beans, New Orleans Style
Red Kidney Beans
Baked Lima Beans with Bacon
Creole Lima Beans
Boiled Lima Beans
Boston Baked Beans
Honey-baked Beans
Buttered Fresh Beets
Buttered Sliced Beets
Harvard Beets
Hot Spiced Beets
Buttered Fresh Broccoli
Broccoli Amandine
Broccoli au Gratin
Broccoli Hollandaise
Broccoli with Cream Sauce
Broccoli with Cheese Sauce
Broccoli with Lemon Butter Sauce
Broccoli Polonaise
Buttered Broccoli
Buttered Brussels Sprouts
Brussels Sprouts au Gratin
Brussels Sprouts in Onion Cream
Brussels Sprouts Hollandaise
Creamed Brussels Sprouts
Buttered Cabbage
Cabbage au Gratin
Chinese Fried Cabbage

Creamed Cabbage
Hot Slaw (Mustard Cabbage)
Princess Cabbage
Red Cabbage Bavarian
Coleslaw
Buttered Diced Carrots
Candied Carrot Strips
Buttered Young Carrots
Carrots Vichyssoise
Glazed Carrots
Carrot Balls
Cheddar Carrots
Creamed Carrots
French-fried Carrots
Lyonnaise Carrots
Buttered Cauliflower
Cauliflower Amandine
Cauliflower, Country Style
Cauliflower Parmesan
Cauliflower Polonaise
Cauliflower au Gratin
Cauliflower Creole
Curried Cauliflower
Braised Cauliflower Greens
Cauliflower Greens au Gratin
Braised Celery
Creamed Celery
Corn on the Cob
Roast Corn
Stewed Corn and Tomatoes
Buttered Corn Kernels
Buttered Succotash
Corn O'Brien
Baked Corn Creole
Corn Pudding
Creamed Corn
Scalloped Corn
Succotash
Baked Eggplant
Eggplant Amandine
Eggplant au gratin
Creole Eggplant

French-fried Eggplant
Buttered Green Beans
Green Beans Lyonnaise
Creamed Green Beans
Creole Green Beans
Curried Green Beans
Green Beans Amandine
Green Beans Sweet-Sour
Piquant Green Beans
Baked Hominy Grits
Buttered Hominy
Hominy Creole
Hominy in Cream
Buttered Kohlrabi
Creamed Kohlrabi
Wilted Lettuce with Croutons
Buttered Mixed Vegetables
Broiled Fresh Mushrooms
Creamed Mushrooms
Fresh Mushrooms Sauté
Sautéed Okra with Cream Sauce
Buttered Okra
Curried Okra
Fried Onions
Glazed Onions
Onions au Gratin
French-fried Onions
Buttered Onions
Buttered Parsnips
Creamed Parsnips
Fried Parsnips
Buttered Peas
Creamed Peas
Curried Peas
Peas with Cheese
Baked Potatoes—Idaho Potatoes
Baked Stuffed Potatoes
Hash-brown Potatoes
Boiled Potatoes
Cottage-fried Potatoes
Scalloped Potatoes
Fluffy Mashed Potatoes

French Baked Potatoes
French-fried Potatoes
Julienne Potatoes
Shoestring Potatoes
Straw Potatoes
Saratoga Chips
Latke Potatoes
Home-fried Potatoes
Potato Chips
Paprika Potatoes
Pan-roasted Potatoes
Oven-browned Potatoes
Parisienne Potatoes
Potatoes Anna
Potato Knish
Potatoes O'Brien
Potato Pancakes
Soufflé Potatoes
Steamed Potatoes
Creamed Potatoes
Parsley Boiled Potatoes
Au Gratin Potatoes
Delmonico Potatoes
Creamed Potatoes with Cheese
Lyonnaise Potatoes
Duchess Potatoes
Fried Potato Cakes
Potato Croquettes
Potato Puffs
Scalloped Potatoes with Onions
Mashed Potatoes
Potatoes au Gratin
Candied Sweet Potatoes
Baked Sweet Potatoes
Boiled Sweet Potatoes
Sherried Sweet Potatoes
Baked Sweet Potatoes and Apples
Mashed Sweet Potatoes in Orange Shell
Sweet Potatoes Baked with Marshmallows
Sweet Potatoes Royale
Sweet Potato Patties with Coconut

Sweet Potato Puffs
Buttered Salsify
Creamed Salsify
Chopped Spinach
Spinach au Gratin
Creamed Spinach
Baked Acorn Squash
Glazed Acorn Squash
Mashed Acorn Squash
Baked Hubbard Squash
Squash Creole
Buttered Squash
Baked Stuffed Tomatoes
French-fried Tomatoes
Fried Tomatoes
Grilled Tomatoes
Stewed Tomatoes
Buttered Turnips
Mashed Turnips
Creamed Turnips

Salads

Apple, Carrot, and Raisin Salad
Waldorf Salad
Avocado and Grape Salad
Banana and Nut Salad
Banana and Orange Salad
Fruit Salad
Grapefruit Salad
Peach and Romaine Salad
Pineapple and Lettuce Salad
Pineapple and Cottage Cheese Salad
Stuffed Date Salad
Pineapple and Cream Cheese Salad
Stuffed Plum Salad
Stuffed Prune Salad
Asparagus and Dandelion Salad
Asparagus and Lettuce Salad
Asparagus and Tomato Salad

Beet Relish
Beet and Chicory Salad
Beet and Cucumber Salad
Beet and Endive Salad
Beet and Watercress Salad
Coleslaw
Cabbage and Carrot Salad
Celery, Olives, and Radishes
Celery and Watercress Salad
Chef's Salad
Tossed Green Salad
Spring Salad
Cucumber and Lettuce Salad
Cucumber and Romaine Salad
Garden Salad
Lettuce, Tomato, and Green Onion Salad
Cottage Cheese Salad
Kidney Bean Salad
Lettuce Salad
Lettuce and Tomato Salad
Macaroni Salad
Pickled Beets
Potato Salad
Salad Relish Tray
Emerald Salad
Jellied Banana and Grape Salad
Jellied Cream Cheese Salad
Jellied Cream Cheese and Pineapple Salad
Jellied Cooked Vegetable Salad
Perfection Salad
Jewel Salad
Sylvia Salad
Tomato Aspic Salad
Chicken Salad
Crabmeat Salad
Egg Salad
Lobster Salad
Salmon Salad
Shrimp Salad
Tuna Fish Salad

Common Salad Dressings

Blue Cheese Dressing
Caesar Dressing
Celery Seed Dressing
Chiffonnade Dressing
Cream Mayonnaise
Cumberland Dressing
Emerald Dressing
French Dressing, Plain
French Dressing, Thick
Fruit Salad Dressing
Golden Fruit Dressing
Italian Oil and Vinegar Dressing
Italian Dressing
Louis Dressing
Mayonnaise
Maple Dressing
Oil and Vinegar Dressing
Prince Dressing
Russian Dressing
Cooked Salad Dressing
Sour Cream Dressing
Thousand Island Dressing
Vinaigrette Dressing

Breads

Rye Bread
Egg Twist Bread
White Bread
Individual Round Loaves
Raisin Bread
Whole Wheat Honey Bread
Whole Wheat Bread
Garlic Toast
Banana Bread
Pan Rolls
Cloverleaf Rolls
Salt Sticks—White, Rye, and Whole Wheat

Crescents—White, Rye, and Whole Wheat
Parker House Rolls
Figure Eights
Bowknots
Rosettes
Braids
Poppy Seed Rolls
Fantans
Finger Rolls
Onion Rolls
Hard Rolls
Gingerbread
Sally Lunn Muffins
Southern Spoon Bread
Scotch Scones
Cinnamon Buns
Butterfly Buns
Honey Buns
Hot Cross Buns
Bear Claws

Desserts

Apple Cake
Peach Cake
Marble Cake
Banana Layer Cake
Boston Cream Pie
Chocolate Marshmallow Layer Cake
Chocolate Walnut Layer Cake
Coconut Layer Cake
Fudge Layer Cake
Lemon Marshmallow Cake
Lady Baltimore Cake
Maple Layer Cake
Mocha Nut Layer Cake
Orange Layer Cake
Pineapple Marshmallow Cake
Sponge Cake
Genoise Cake

Lemon Sponge Cake
Orange Sponge Cake
Strawberry Shortcake
Petits Fours
Pineapple Cake
Chiffon Cake
Jelly Roll
Fruit Cake
Spice Cake
Pound Cake
Pound Cake with Fruits
Pound Cake with Raisins
Cheese Cake
Cream Puffs (Vanilla Cream)
Cream Puffs (Chantilly Cream)
Chocolate Glaze
French Doughnuts
Meringue Floating Island
Meringue Kisses
Fresh Blackberry Pie
Fresh Blueberry Pie
Fresh Raspberry Pie
Canned Cherry Pie
Fresh Apple Pie
Dutch Apple Pie
Apricot Whip Pie
Raisin Pie
Custard Pie
Pineapple Custard Pie
Pumpkin Pie
Lemon Meringue Pie
Banana Cream Pie
Cherry Cream Pie
Chocolate Cream Pie
Date and Nut Cream Pie
Strawberry Cream Pie
Chocolate Chiffon Pie
Lemon Chiffon Pie
Lime Chiffon Pie
Pineapple Chiffon Pie
Apple Cobbler

Apricot Cobbler
Peach Cobbler
Blueberry-Blackberry Cobbler
Fresh Blueberry Tart
Cherry Tart
Chiffon Tart
Chocolate Cream Tart
Peach Tart
Fresh Strawberry Tart
Vanilla Tart
Lemon Sponge Pudding
Baked Custard
Graham Cracker Pudding
Caramel Cup Custard
Baked Custard with Cherry Sauce
French Custard Pudding
Blancmange
Blancmange with Crushed Fruit
Cream of Peach Pudding
Butterscotch Pudding
Chocolate Pudding
Cream of Pineapple Pudding
Vanilla Pudding with Whipped Cream
Pineapple Cream Pudding
Bread Pudding
Chocolate Bread Pudding
Apple Brown Betty
Fresh Fruit Cake Pudding
Apple Scallop
Peach Scallop
Fresh Pineapple Fluff
Almond Farina Pudding
Steamed Blueberry Pudding
Cherry Delight
Apple Delight
Apricot Delight
Pineapple Delight
Creamy Tapioca Pudding
Fresh Fruit Tapioca
Apple Tapioca Pudding
Lemon Tapioca Pudding
Creamed Raisin-Rice Pudding

Custard Rice Pudding
Fig Condé
Apricot Condé
Roquefort
Camembert
Gruyère
Fresh Fruit Gelatin
Apple, Apricot, Prune Bavarian Cream
Gelatin Cubes with Whipped Cream
Lemon Snow Pudding
Orange Charlotte
Spanish Cream
Pineapple Marshmallow Fluff
Iced Cantaloupe
Iced Casaba Melon
Iced Honey Ball
Iced Watermelon
Fresh Berries
Fresh Peaches
Fresh Pineapple
Fresh Strawberries Romanoff
Strawberry Flambè
Baked Apples
Baked Apple Quarters
Baked Rhubarb
Fruit Compote
Stewed Apples
Stewed Red Cherries
Spiced Peaches
Stewed Fresh Plums
Stewed Dried Apricots
Stewed Prunes
Banana Float
Blackberry Float
Peach Float
Baked Apple Crisp
Baked Peach Crisp
Apricot Whip
Chocolate Whip
Fresh Peach Whip
Pineapple Whip
Prune Whip

Vanilla Ice Cream
Banana Ice Cream
Chocolate Ribbon Ice Cream
Peach Ice Cream
Strawberry Ice Cream
French Ice Cream
Lemon Sherbet
Orange Sherbet
Pineapple Sherbet
Raspberry Sherbet
Biscuit Tortoni
Nut Sundaes
Fruit Sundaes
Pie a la Mode
Parfaits
Ice Cream Whips
Ice Cream Eclair

DINNER

Appetizers

California Ripe Olives
Chilled Tomato Juice Cocktail
Fresh Crabmeat Canapé
Supreme of Grapefruit Maraschino
Little Neck Clams
Carrot and Celery Juice
Homemade Antipasto with Anchovies
Iced Natural Grape Juice
Bluepoint Oyster Cocktail
Fresh Fruit Cup, Melba
Sunrayed Tomato Juice Cocktail
Assorted Hors d'Oeuvres
California Fruit Juice
Eggs Stuffed with Mushrooms in Jelly
Chilled Honeydew Melon
Iced Clam Juice
Orange Mint Cup
Smoked Salmon Cornet with Horseradish
Hawaiian Pineapple Juice

Hot Cheese Canapé
Beet Stuffed with Egg Salad
Cherrystone Clam Cocktail
Chilled Loganberry Juice
Hot Deviled Sardine Canapé
Minted Apple Juice
Fresh Shrimp Cocktail
Iced Sauerkraut Juice
Avocado Pear Cocktail
Fresh Fruit Cup with Orange Sherbet
Shredded Ham with Chopped Olives
Eggs Stuffed with Chicken Livers
Italian Antipasto
Fresh Crabmeat Cocktail
Iced Cherry Juice
Bluepoint Oyster Cocktail
Iced California Plum Juice
Stuffed Celery
Yellow Tomato Juice Cocktail
Marinated Herring
Deviled Ham Canapé
Hot Sausage Roll
Imported Boneless Sardines
Sliced Eggs with Thousand Island Dressing
Texas Pink Grapefruit Half
Bismarck Herring
Mixed Fresh Seafood Cocktail
Deviled Egg on Shredded Lettuce
Anchovy Canapé
Julienned Tongue on Coleslaw
Celery and Olives
Eggs Stuffed with Red Caviar
Assorted Canapés
Chicken Liver Canapé
Fresh Lobster and Crabmeat in Jelly
Carrot Relish
Celery Relish
Horseradish Relish
Algerian Relish
Beet and Celery Relish
Pickled, Spiced, or Stuffed Beets
Spiced Watermelon or Honeydew Rind

Spiced Pineapple
Spiced Peaches, Peach Chutney
Orange and Cranberry Relish
Egg and Celery Relish
Beef Relish
Cucumber Relish
Russian Salad
Brandied Dates
Salted Nuts, Pickled Walnuts
Chow Chow, Mustard Pickles
Radish Roses
Sliced Tomatoes
Sliced Cucumbers
Palm Hearts
Pickled Onions
Artichoke Hearts (in oil with cold mustard dressing)
Sliced Egg with Hartford Sauce
Sliced Egg on Shredded or Julienned Ham or Tongue with Thousand Island Dressing
Sliced Egg on Smoked Salmon with Russian or Horseradish Dressing
Stuffed Eggs with Sardine Butter
Eggs in Aspic
Cucumber Cup Stuffed with Crab Meat
Beet Cup Stuffed with Anchovies
Stuffed Tomato Surprise with Shrimp
Marinated Herring
Herring in Wine or with Cream
Italian Antipasto
Imported Sturgeon
Eels in Jelly
Fillets of Imported Anchovies
Imported Norwegian Brisling
Italian Salami, Sausage, and Liverwurst
Westphalian Ham
Ham Cornet with Coleslaw or Watercress
Smoked Salmon Cornet with Caviar, Horseradish, Watercress, etc.
Salami Cornet with Watercress, Coleslaw, Chopped Pickles
Julienne of Salami, Ham, or Tongue with Chopped Olives, Coleslaw

Smoked Salmon
Pickled Salmon
Salmon in Jelly
Mackerel in White Wine
Smoked Turkey
Cheese and Olives
Crabmeat Washington
Lobster Lorenzo
Crab Lorenzo
Deviled Sardines
Finnan Haddie
Monte Cristo
Chopped Beef and Bacon Rolls
Broiled Olives in Bacon
Oyster and Bacon Curls
Shad Roe in Bacon Curls
Scallop and Bacon Curls
Tuna Fish Balls
Corned Beef Hash Balls with or without Chili or Savory Sauce
Mushroom Rolls
Eggplant Julienne
Viennoise Hors d'Oeuvres
Rissolette
Cocktail Sausages
Cheese Cigarettes
Artichoke Bottom, Greek Style
Blini (Russian Pancakes Served with Caviar Cheese)
Codfish Cake (like small Cocktail Sausages)

Soups

Jellied Madrilène
Jellied Consommé
Jellied Gumbo
Jellied Bouillon
Jellied Tomato Bouillon
Jellied Consommé Riche
Jellied Bourbonnaise
Jellied Cyrano
Cold Russian Borsch

Cold Beef Broth
Cold Russian Klodnick
Cold Russian Botvinya
Cold Cream Vichyssoise
Cold Cherry Soup
Cold Mexican Avocado Pear Soup
Cold Swedish Fruit Tapioca
Cold Florida Consommé
Cream of Fresh Peas
Cream of Onions
Cream of Fresh Spinach
Cream of Almonds
Cream of Fresh Cauliflower
Cream of Fresh Mushrooms
Cream of Sorrel
Cream of Tomato
Cream of Barley
Cream of Brussels Sprouts
Cream of Fresh Beet Greens or Young Beets
Cream of Chicory
Cream of Watercress
Cream of Celery
Cream of Fresh Corn (Corn Chatelaine)
Cream of Potato
Cream of Fresh Vegetable
Cream of Carrot
Cream of Rice
Cream of Tapioca
Cream of Lettuce (Lettuce Corneille)
Cream of String Bean (String Bean Therese)
Cream of Artichoke
Cream of Canadian Cheese Soup
Crayfish Bisque
Crabmeat Bisque
Scallop Bisque
Lobster Bisque
Shrimp Bisque
Clam Bisque
Oyster Bisque
Manhattan Clam Chowder

Rhode Island Clam Chowder
New England Clam Chowder
Maine Clam Chowder
Cape Cod Clam Chowder
Oyster Chowder
Virginia Oyster Chowder or Soup
Oyster and Corn Chowder
Boston Fish Chowder
Connecticut Fish Chowder
Potage of Mussels
Bouillabaisse
Oyster, Crabmeat, and Shrimp Gumbo
Shrimp Chowder
Kalaloo (West Indies fish soup with ham, okra, and spinach)
Salmon, Halibut, or Carp Soup
Corn Chowder
Bean Chowder
Vegetable Chowder
Okra Gumbo
Spring Vegetable Soup
Plantation Style Vegetable Soup
Italian Vegetable Soup
Oxtail Soup
Navy Bean Soup
Red Kidney Soup
Lentil or German Lentil Soup
Scotch Broth with Barley
Russian Cabbage Soup
Cock-a-leekie
Brown Mushroom Soup
Potage Santé (Brown Stock with Mashed Carrots and Egg Yolk)
Potage Garure (with Onions, Cabbage, etc.)
Potage Jackson
Potage Excelsior
Potage Crécy
Olla Podrida (Spanish Soup, very thick, with Chick Peas, Ham Sausage, etc.)
Mexican Puchero Soup
Tomato and Cabbage Soup

Tomato Gumbo
Potage a la Russe (Brown Stock with Vegetables and Sausage Balls)
Potage a la Bonne Femme (Half Stock and Milk, Potatoes, Leeks, French Bread)
Potage Ancienne (Famous French Peasant Soup with Beef, Vegetables and Chicken)
Turkey Soup
Duck Soup

Entrees: Fish

Broiled Bluefish
Butterfish Sauté
Broiled Butterfish
Poached Cod
Codfish in Cream with Pimento and Hard-cooked Eggs
Steamed Haddock
Poached Haddock
Baked Haddock Steak
Stuffed Haddock Steak with Mushrooms
Creamed Haddock
Broiled Haddock Fillets
Fillet of Sole, Fried
Baked Sole
Poached Sole
Broiled Sole
Fillet of Sole Yacht Club
Fillet of Sole Bonne Femme
Fillet of Sole Montreuil
Fried Halibut
Broiled Halibut Steak
Poached Halibut Steak
Baked Halibut Steak
Poached Halibut Ménagère
Broiled Mackerel
Baked Mackerel
Baked Salmon
Broiled Salmon Steak
Poached or Steamed Salmon

Cold Salmon with Ravigote
Salmon Loaf
Salmon Cutlets
Salmon Soufflé
Salmon Salad
Baked Shad
Broiled Shad Fillets
Shad Croquettes
Broiled Swordfish
Baked Swordfish
Broiled Trout
Baked Trout
Poached Trout
Trout au Gratin
Scalloped Trout
Trout Croquettes
Trout a la King
Steamed Clams
Clam Fritters
Clams Baked in Shell
Broiled Oysters
Deviled Oysters
Fried Oysters
Oysters au Gratin
Scalloped Oysters with Macaroni
Oyster Fritters
Oysters Baltimore with Madeira Sauce
Baked Oysters Victor
Baked Oysters Ravigote
Baked Oysters on Toast, American Style
Baked Oysters Casino
Oyster Stew
Baked Oysters with Chives
Special Assorted Baked Oyster Plate
Oysters en Brochette with Bacon and Maitre d'Hotel Butter
Fried Shrimp
Shrimp au Gratin
Shrimp Curry and Rice
Deviled Crab
Fried Crabmeat
Broiled Crabmeat

Crab Mornay
Crab Newburg
Crab a la King
Crab au Gratin
Broiled Lobster
Boiled Lobster
Baked Lobster
Creamed Lobster
Lobster Newburg
Lobster au Gratin
Lobster Mornay
Lobster Thermidor
Fried Frogs' Legs
Broiled Frogs' Legs
Frogs' Legs au Gratin

Beef

Pineapple Beef Patty Wrapped in Bacon
Chopped Beef Steak Stanley with Sautéed Bananas and Horseradish Sauce
Chopped Beef Steak Grilled on Sizzling Platter
Hamburger Steak on Onion Rings or with Onion Sauce
Chopped Sautéed Beef and Mushroom Steak with Mushroom Gravy
Chopped Jumbo Beef Steak Sautéed in Sweet Butter
Grilled Chopped Choice Beef Steak with French Fried Onions
Beef Patty off the Charcoal Broiler
Beef Chop Suey with Steamed Rice
Chili con Carne with Red Kidney Beans
Beef Curry with Steamed Rice
Potted Beef and Mushrooms en Casserole
Pepper Steak with Green Peppers and Fresh Mushrooms
Sirloin Tips en Casserole with Eggplant and Parisienne Potatoes
Oxtail Ragout en Casserole
Beef en Casserole with Fresh Vegetables
Beef Kidney Stew, Maryland Style
Chopped Beef and Noodles en Casserole
Swiss Steak with Dumplings

Roulade of Beef with Mixed Fresh Vegetables
Flank Steak, New Orleans Style
Potted Steak with Mushrooms, Boston Style
Swiss Steak, Maryland Style
Barbecued Short Ribs, Western Style
Prime Beef Short Ribs with Natural Gravy
Braised Beef Short Ribs with Onion or Barbecue Sauce
Boiled Beef with Horseradish, Vinaigrette, or Creole Sauce
Corned Brisket of Beef and New Cabbage
Boiled New England Dinner
Beef a la Mode with Carrots and Onions
Prime Ribs of Beef with Natural Gravy
Boned Rib Roast with Yorkshire Pudding and Pan Gravy
Tenderloin-In Fillet of Beef
Beef a la Mode
Yankee Pot Roast
German Pot Roast
Sauerbraten with Potato Pancakes
Beef Stroganoff with Sour Cream
Top Sirloin of Beef
Beef a la Deutsch
Corned Beef
Casserole of Beef
Beef Pie
Meat Loaf
Beef Cutlets
Beef Salad
Beef a la Mode in Jelly
Beef Stew

Lamb and Mutton

Roast Leg of Spring Lamb
Roast Stuffed Spring Lamb
Roast Crown of Lamb
Roast Saddle of Lamb or Mutton
Braised Leg or Shoulder of Lamb with Bretonne Beans
Roast or Boiled Leg of Mutton with Caper Sauce
Braised Shoulder of Lamb Stuffed with Special Savory Dressing

Braised Breast of Lamb
Breast of Lamb Maryland with Corn Fritters, Bacon, and Cream Sauce
Smothered Breast of Lamb, Charleston Style
Barbecued Ribs of Lamb
Chopped Lamb Steak off the Grill with Black Current Jelly
Grilled Lamb Chops
Grilled Mutton Chops
Irish Lamb Stew with Dumplings
Lamb Curry with Steamed Rice
Lamb Stew (Browned Stew)
Ragout of Lamb, Southern Style
Lamb en Casserole
Fricassee of Spring Lamb
Casserole of Rice Ring and Lamb
Baked Lamb Hash with Green Peppers
Lamb with Barbecue Sauce
Lamb Cutlets
Lamb au Gratin

Veal

Roast Veal
Braised Leg of Veal
Roast or Braised Loin of Veal
Roast Stuffed Shoulder of Veal
Braised Stuffed Cushion of Veal
Breaded Veal Chops
Veal Cutlets
Veal Cutlets Sautéed in Paprika Sauce
Stuffed Veal Cutlets, Viennese Style
Veal Chops or Cutlets en Casserole
Veal Sauté Marengo with Tomatoes and Fresh Mushrooms
Stuffed Veal Rolls with Fresh Spinach
Spanish Veal Balls with Tomato Sauce
Ragout of Milk-fed Veal
Veal Stew with Fresh Vegetables
Curry of Veal with Steamed Rice
Veal Birds (Thin Slices of Leg Stuffed, Rolled, Sautéed, or en Casserole with Cream Sauce)
Veal en Casserole with Small Onions and Potato Balls

Smothered Breast of Veal a la Charleston
Veal Goulash with Paprika Sauce
Veal a la King
Scalloped Veal
Blanquette of Veal
Mixed Veal on Toast
Veal Shortcake
Sautéed Veal and Green Peppers
Veal and Ham Pie
Cold Sliced Veal
Veal in Jelly
Veal Loaf with Tomato, Cream, or Mushroom Sauce
Veal Croquettes with Cream Sauce
Veal Chow Mein
Veal Fritters French Style with Tomato Sauce
Casserole of Veal and Rice
Creamed Veal and Celery
Veal Supreme, Tomato or Mushroom Sauce

Pork and Ham

Baked Clay County, Kentucky, Ham with Cherry Sauce
Spiced Southern Ham with Cider Sauce
Roast Sugar-cured Ham, Hawaiian Style
Baked Candied Virginia Ham with Burgundy Sauce
Glazed Wiltshire Ham, Southern Style, with Champagne Sauce
Baked Premium Ham with Orange Sauce
The Original West Virginia Ham with Glazed Fruits
Special Sugar-cured Beechnut Ham with Mustard Sauce
Baked Genuine Smithfield, Virginia Ham with Oscar Sauce
Braised York Ham with Madeira Sauce
Imported Hungarian Ham with Tokay Wine Sauce
Barbecued Cottage Ham with Barbecue Sauce
Baked Glazed Tennessee Ham with Raisin Sauce
Southern Peanut-fed Baked Ham with Godard Sauce
Baked Honey-cured Ham with Sautéed Pineapple Ring
Baked Hickory-smoked Ham with Cumberland Sauce
Crown Roast of Pork
Roast Stuffed Suckling Pig
Grilled Pork Chops
Breaded Pork Chops

Grilled Ham Steak
Pork Tenderloin Steak
Baked Stuffed Pork Chops
Ragout of Fresh Pork, Hungarian Style, with Egg Noodles
Spareribs and Cabbage
Roast Stuffed Spareribs
Barbecued Spareribs
Baked Spareribs en Casserole with Vegetables
Pork and Beans
Fried Salt Pork, Country Style
Southern Ham Loaf
Scalloped Sausage and Macaroni
Pork a la King
Ham, Sweet Potato, and Pineapple Patties
Ham Soufflé
Ham Omelet
Ham Croquettes
Scalloped Ham and Potatoes
Ham au Gratin
Ham and Sweet Potato Fritters
Ham and Macaroni en Casserole

Chicken

Chicken Stanley with Sautéed Bananas
Smothered Half Chicken, Swedish Style
Boned Stuffed Chicken Leg
Chicken Fricassee with Steamed Rice
Chicken Stew with Dumplings
Southern Fried Chicken with Cream Sauce
Chicken Curry with Steamed Rice
Chicken Pot Pie with Biscuit Cover
Chicken Stew, Mexican Style
Braised Chicken
Chicken Paprika, Creole, etc.
Chicken en Brochette with Mushrooms or Tomatoes
Broiled or Sautéed Chicken
Mixed Chicken Liver Grill
Chicken Livers en Casserole with Rice Plate
Broiled Chicken Livers on Toast with Bacon Strips

Chicken Liver Grill with Mushrooms, Tomato, Eggplant, Ham, and Potatoes
Chicken a la King in Patty Shell
Chicken Vol-au-vent with Sweetbreads
Creamed Chicken Aurora
Creamed Chicken on Toasted Corn Bread
Creamed Chicken and Oysters Metropole
Chicken and Ham a la King
Chicken Chow Mein
Chicken Roll in Biscuit Crust with Mushroom Sauce
Brunswick Chicken Stew with Corn and Fresh Lima Beans
Baked Pancake Stuffed with Creamed Chicken au Gratin
Chicken Barbecue
Chicken Cutlets
Chicken Pot Pie with Flaky Pastry Cover

Turkey

Turkey Tetrazzini
Turkey Hash, Charleston Style
Scalloped Turkey en Casserole
Turkey Cake with Celery Cream Sauce
Roast Stuffed Turkey with Dressing
Turkey a la King

Duck

Roast Stuffed Duck with Orange, Bigarade Sauce
Duck and Rice Pilaf, Savannah Style
Duck Cutlets
Duck Curry with Steamed Rice
Royal Squab

Vegetables and Potatoes

Mushrooms a la King with Cooked Eggs on Toast
Peas and Mushrooms en Casserole
Peas, Onions, Mushrooms, and Celery en Casserole
Peas, Baby Carrots, Small Onions, and Salt Pork en Casserole

Chopped Beets and Spinach with Bacon Dressing
Scalloped Eggplant with Tomatoes, Bread, and Green Peppers
Creamed String Beans and Sautéed Onions
Braised Brussels Sprouts and Chestnuts
Cauliflower with Chopped Sautéed Onions or Mushrooms and
Brown Butter
Succotash with Tomatoes, Onion, and Garlic
Curried Mixed Vegetables
Buttered Green Peas
Grilled Tomatoes
Braised Carrots
Purée of Spinach
Broiled Mushrooms
Baked Stuffed Potato
String Beans Maitre d'Hotel
Broccoli Hollandaise
Harvard Beets
Baked Squash
Celery with Grated Cheese
Riced Potatoes
French-fried Eggplant
Buttered Baby Lima Beans
Spinach with Bacon Dressing
Stringless Beans, Poulette
Glazed Onions
New Buttered Cabbage
Creamed Spinach
Baked Young Beets
Sautéed Tomatoes
Rissole Potato
Baked Idaho Potato
Brussels Sprouts, Brown Butter
Garden Spinach, French Style
Parisienne Peas
Red Cabbage
Creamed Baby Carrots
Buttered String Beans
New Young Corn on the Cob
Grilled Tomato
Baked Zucchini
Parsley Potatoes
Pan-roasted Potatoes

French-fried Potatoes
Long Branch Potatoes
Pont Neuf Potatoes
Hashed-brown Potatoes
Home-fried Potatoes
Potato Pancakes
Potatoes Duchesse
Stuffed Potato Bohemienne
Stuffed Potato a la Swiss
Parsley Potatoes
Pan-roasted Potato
Mashed Potatoes
Baked Sweet Potatoes
Mashed Sweet Potatoes
Stuffed Sweet Potatoes
Imperial Sweet Potatoes
Scalloped Sweet Potatoes with Apple
Sweet Potato Balls
Sweet Potato O'Brien
Sweet Potatoes Deluxe with Pineapple and Almonds
Artichokes Hollandaise
Stuffed Artichokes
Asparagus au Gratin
Broccoli Mousseline
Brussels Sprouts with Chestnuts
Brussels Sprouts, Italian Style
Braised Cabbage
Chinese Cabbage
Cauliflower Milanaise
Cauliflower Mousseline
Corn Fritters
Corn Pudding
Buttered Cucumber
Eggplant, French Fried
Stuffed Eggplant
Buttered Lima Beans
Mushrooms a la King
French-fried Onions
Oyster Plant au Gratin
Fried Parsnips
Parsnip Fritters

Creamed Peas
Boiled Peas
Baked Pumpkin
Mashed Pumpkin
Baked Squash
Stuffed Squash
Squash, Milanese Style
Julienne String Beans
Swiss Chard with Brown Butter
Swiss Chard au Gratin
Tomatoes Hollandaise
Mashed Turnips
Zucchini with Tomatoes, Milanaise Style

Salads

Spring Salad: Tomato, Cucumber, and Radish (Sliced)
Green Pepper (Julienned) Green Salad or Spring Onions with French Dressing
Mixed Vegetable Salad with Cooked Peas, Beets, Carrots, etc., with Mayonnaise or French Dressing and Chopped Parsley
Mixed Vegetable Salad with Cooked Cauliflower, Asparagus Tips, etc., with Chiffonnade Dressing
Florentine Salad: Diced Celery, Endive, Cucumber on Lettuce with Chiffonnade Dressing
Julienned Tomatoes, Celery, Beets, or Chicory with French Dressing and Fine Herbs
Tomato and Celery Salad
Tomato, Celery, and Green Pepper Salad
Tomato and Cucumber Salad on Crisp Lettuce with Swedish Mayonnaise
Tomato and Watercress Salad with Chopped Fresh Herbs and French Dressing
Tomato and Bermuda Onion on Mixed Salad Greens with Piquant Dressing
Tomato Stuffed with Cottage Cheese and Chives
Egg Salad
Cucumber Salad
Macaroni Salad
Potato Salad
Fresh Shrimp Salad

Crabmeat or Lobster Salad
Chicken and Fresh Vegetable Salad
Tuna Fish or Salmon Salad
Cream Cheese and Olive Salad
Ham and Chicken Salad
Ham Salad
Tongue Salad
Veal Salad
Coleslaw
Biarritz Salad
Field Salad
Health Salad
Dutch Cabbage Slaw
Melon Ring Filled with Diced Fresh Pineapple, Topped with Orange Sections
Melon Ring Filled with Mixed Fresh Fruit Salad
Grapefruit, Orange, and Avocado Pear Salad
Fresh Fruit Salad
Orange and Grapefruit Salad Separated by Green Pepper or Romaine
Apple and Celery Salad
Tango Salad
Brazilian Salad
Hungarian Fruit Salad
Fan Fruit Salad

Breads: Quick Breads—Biscuit Type

Cinnamon Rolls
Cheese Biscuits
Drop Biscuits
Orange Biscuits
Peanut Butter Biscuits
Cream of Tartar Biscuits

Quick Breads—Loaf Type

Apricot and Raisin Bread
Banana Bread
Brown Bread
Cherry Nut Bread

Dark Nut Bread
Date Bread
Gingerbread
Nut Bread
Nut and Raisin Bread
Orange and Raisin Bread
Pecan Bread

Quick Breads and Muffins

Bacon
Banana
Corn
Cranberry
Dark Brown
Ginger
Graham
Jelly
Maple
Oatmeal
Sweet Rye
Currant
Dark Brown
Date
Date and Nut
Grapenut
Orange
Pineapple
Prune Bran
Rye
Strawberry
Popovers
Honey

Yeast Bread

Cracked Wheat
Graham
Nut
Oatmeal
Sweet Rye

White
Raisin
Raisin, Spiced
Old-fashioned Rye
Salt Rising
Whole Wheat
Pumpernickel

Rolls

Bran
Butterfluff
Cheese
Cracked Wheat
Cloverleaf
Cornmeal
Cottage
Crescent
Dinner
Finger
French
Graham
Hard
Oatmeal
Pan
Parker House
Poppy Seed
Rye

Desserts

Mississippi Pecan Pie
Apple Pie
Pumpkin Pie
Butterscotch Pie
Almond Pie
Chocolate Pie
Custard Pie
Pineapple Pie
Fresh Coconut Cream Pie
Strawberry Pie

White Layer Cake
Rich White Cake
Angel Slice Supreme, Served with Raspberry or Orange Ice
Macaroon Delight with Raspberry Ice
Brown Fingers a la Mode
Jelly Roll Special with Ice Cream
Toasted Cake Praline with Vanilla Ice Cream
Brownie Points a la Mode
Chocolate Ice Cream Surprise
Old-fashioned Rice Pudding
Pineapple Rice Cream
Peaches with Melba Sauce
Indian Pudding
Date Dessert with Whipped Cream
Fresh Fruit Compote
Prune Whip
Apricot Whip
Fresh Blueberry Pie
Maple Layer Cake
Old-fashioned Strawberry Shortcake
Iced Watermelon
Orange Bavarian Cream
Cake a la Mode with Black Cherry Rum Sauce
Stewed Fresh Apricots
Fresh Strawberries with Cream
Ice Cream with Fresh Pineapple Sauce
Fresh Blackberry Pie
Chocolate Layer Cake
Fresh Strawberry Tart
Compote of Fresh Fruits
Lemon Meringue Pie
Slice Fresh Pineapple
Fresh Apricot Cobbler
Frozen Burnt Almond Pie
Tru-Blu-Berries with Cream
Meringue Shell with Ice Cream and Fresh Raspberry Sauce
Old-fashioned Rice Pudding a la Mode
Ice Cream with Fresh Cherry Sauce
Choice of Fresh Peach, Vanilla, Spumoni, or Fresh Strawberry Ice Cream
Choice of Bel Paese, Philadelphia Cream, Imported Roquefort, Camembert, or Gorgonzola Cheese with Toasted Crackers

Apple Brown Betty with Lemon Sauce
Apricot Betty
Bread Pudding
Banana Bread Pudding
Apple Scallop
Creamed Rice Pudding
Apple Batter Pudding
Lemon Dessert Pudding
Cinnamon Apple Cupcake
Gingerbread with Whipped Cream
Blueberry Cottage Pudding
Banana Shortcake with Whipped Cream
Orange Shortcake with Hard Sauce
Strawberry Shortcake with Whipped Cream
Apricot and Date Upside-down Cake
Fresh Fruit Roll with Fruit Sauce
Apple Fritters with Cinnamon
Banana Fritters with Fruit Sauce
Pineapple Fritters with Lemon Sauce
Plum Pudding
Carrot Pudding
Christmas Pudding with Brandy Sauce
Apple Tapioca Pudding
Caramel Custard
Chocolate Custard Pudding
Coconut Cup
Floating Island with Bananas
Almond Macaroon Pudding
Apricot Mold with Almonds
Fruit Jelly
Ginger Cranberry
Baked Apple
Apples Stewed with Slices of Lemon
Apricot and Fig Sauce
Baked Bananas
Baked Pears
Stewed Prunes
Baked Rhubarb
Fresh:
Apples
Oranges
Apricots

Bananas
Peaches
Grapefruit
Mangoes
Melon
Papaya
Honeydew Melon

MENU TERMS

a la **Fr.**	With, or in the fashion of.
a la carte **Fr.**	Not part of a complete meal; usually prepared to order.
a la mode **Fr.**	In desserts, with ice cream; when applied to beef, it means cooked in water with vegetables.
a la Newburg **Fr.**	A creamed dish, with egg yolk added, flavored with sherry; generally used with seafood.
amandine **Fr.**	Served with almonds.
au gratin **Fr.**	With a cheese sauce.
au jus **Fr.**	Natural meat juices, not thickened.
au beurre **Fr.**	Buttered.
bisque **Fr.**	Thick cream soup made from shellfish; may also be a frozen dessert.
bordelaise **Fr.**	Sauce bordelaise is a sauce made with Bordeaux wine; used with meat.
bouillabaisse **Fr.**	Highly seasoned fish and shellfish soup seasoned with herbs.
brioche **Fr.**	A sweetened, rich bread.
canapé **Fr.**	Hot or cold appetizer served on toasted bread or crackers.
carte **Fr.**	Bill of fare or menu; a la carte means according to the bill of fare, and carte du jour is the menu of the day.
du jour **Fr.**	Ready to serve (literally, of the day).
de la maison **Fr.**	Specialty of the house.
entrecote **Fr.**	Steak cut from between the ribs.
entrée **Fr.**	Main course.
espagnole **Fr.**	Spanish; usually refers to brown sauce.
fondu **Fr.**	Melted or blended.
glacé **Fr.**	Glazed or frosted.
gumbo	Creole soup with okra and rice.
hors d'oevre **Fr.**	Relish served at the beginning of a meal in small portions.
jardinière **Fr.**	Served with mixed vegetables.
julienne **Fr.**	Vegetables cut into fine strips.
kosher	Jewish term applied to food prepared in accordance with orthodox Jewish dietary laws.

lyonnaise Fr.	Seasoned with onion and parsley.
macedoine Fr.	Mixture, usually applied to vegetables or fruit.
maitre d'hotel Fr.	Steward; when applied to cooking terms, it refers to parsley lemon butter sauce.
marinade Fr.	A French dressing or pickling solution.
milanaise Fr.	From Milan; generally refers to the use of macaroni cooked with a white sauce and Parmesan cheese.
normande Fr.	From Normandy; suggests the use of whipped cream.
pâté Fr.	Paste or dough; often a paste made from poultry liver.
petits fours Fr.	Small, decorated fancy cakes with fondant frosting.
piquant Fr.	Highly seasoned.
polonaise Fr.	In the Polish style; refers to the use of breadcrumbs, chopped hard-cooked egg, butter, and chopped parsley as a garnish.
purée Fr.	Food that was pulverized or rubbed through a sieve.
ragout Fr.	Type of stew.
ramekin	A individual baking dish.
rissolé Fr.	Browned.
table d'hote Fr.	Literally, table of the host; refers in menu planning to the meal planned by the establishment at a set price.

INDEX

I have been doing part time catering for the last year. - also I cant spell!